T0305912

City Integration and Tourism Development in the Greater Bay Area, China

City Integration and Tourism Development in the Greater Bay Area, China explores the tourism development related issues of city integration in the Greater Bay Area (GBA).

This book starts with a general introduction to the background of the Greater Bay Area in China. Chapter 2 is a historical review, focusing on tourism development in GBA. Chapter 3 introduces the concept of city integration and the profile of GBA. Chapter 4 discusses the effect of city integration on tourism development. Chapter 5 describes the trends of city integration and tourism. Lastly, Chapter 6 is a case study with recommendations for city destination management.

This book is a valuable resource for social science researchers and those in related fields, such as city planners and tourism officers. This book is recommend reading for advanced undergraduate or postgraduate students of urban tourism, tourism economics, and tourism management.

Jian Ming Luo is an Associate Professor in the Faculty of International Tourism and Management at City University of Macau. He has extensive international and multinational tourism working experience. His teaching and research interests focus on urbanization, tourism development, entertainment, and consumer behaviour.

Chi Fung Lam worked in several hospitality and tourism industries in a few different countries including Hong Kong and Canada. His research area focuses on tourism demand analysis and economic impacts. His recent publications have appeared in highly prestigious international academic journals.

Routledge Focus on Tourism and Hospitality

Routledge Focus on Tourism and Hospitality presents small books on big topics and how they intersect with the world of tourism and hospitality research. The idea is to fill the gap between journal article and book. This new short form series offers both established and early-career academics the flexibility to publish cutting-edge commentary on key areas of tourism and hospitality, topical issues, policy-focused research, analytical or theoretical innovations, a summary of the key players or short topics for specialized audiences in a succinct way.

World Heritage and Tourism
Marketing and Management
Bailey Ashton Adie

Tourism and Urban Regeneration
Processes Compressed in Time and Space
Alberto Amore

Tourism, Sanctions and Boycotts
Siamak Seyfi and C. Michael Hall

City Integration and Tourism Development in the Greater Bay Area, China
Jian Ming Luo and Chi Fung Lam

For more information about this series, please visit:
www.routledge.com/tourism/series/FTH

City Integration and Tourism Development in the Greater Bay Area, China

Jian Ming Luo and Chi Fung Lam

Routledge
Taylor & Francis Group

LONDON AND NEW YORK

First published 2020
by Routledge
2 Park Square, Milton Park, Abingdon, Oxon OX14 4RN

and by Routledge
52 Vanderbilt Avenue, New York, NY 10017

Routledge is an imprint of the Taylor & Francis Group, an informa business

British Library Cataloguing-in-Publication Data
A catalogue record for this book is available from the British Library

Library of Congress Cataloging-in-Publication Data
Names: Luo, Jian Ming, author. | Lam, Chi Fung, author.
Title: City integration and tourism development in the Greater Bay Area, China / Jian Ming Luo and Chi Fung Lam.
Description: Abingdon, Oxon ; New York, NY : Routledge, 2020. | Includes bibliographical references and index.
Identifiers: LCCN 2020005516 (print) | LCCN 2020005517 (ebook) | ISBN 9780367259532 (hardback) | ISBN 9780367505332 (paperback) | ISBN 9780429290725 (ebook)
Subjects: LCSH: City planning–China–Guangdong Sheng. | City planning–China–Hong Kong. | City planning–China–Macau (Special Administrative Region) | Regional planning–China–Guangdong Sheng. | Regional planning–China–Hong Kong. | Regional planning–China–Macau (Special Administrative Region) | Tourism–China–Guangdong Sheng–Planning. | Tourism–China–Hong Kong–Planning. | Tourism–China–Macau (Special Administrative Region)–Planning.
Classification: LCC HT169.C62 G7865 2020 (print) | LCC HT169.C62 (ebook) | DDC 307.1/21609512–dc23

LC record available at https://lccn.loc.gov/2020005516

LC ebook record available at https://lccn.loc.gov/2020005517

ISBN: 978-0-367-25953-2 (hbk)
ISBN: 978-0-429-29072-5 (ebk)

Typeset in Times New Roman
by Wearset Ltd, Boldon, Tyne and Wear

Contents

Figures

Tables

Preface

The Guangdong–Hong Kong–Macao Greater Bay Area (GBA) comprises Hong Kong, Macau, and nine municipalities in Guangdong. The nine municipalities are Guangzhou, Shenzhen, Zhuhai, Foshan, Huizhou, Dongguan, Zhongshan, Jiangmen, and Zhaoqing. The key focus of the Greater Bay Area is to enhance, extend, and deepen cooperation between Guangdong, Hong Kong, and Macau by leveraging the comparative advantage of all cities in the Greater Bay Area. State rescaling has become a crucial tool to explain urban and regional restructuring. The rescaling of the state and privileging of city-regions are percieved to be part and parcel of neoliberal agendas to position major cities and strategic city-regions within global circuits of capital accumulation.

On the one hand, the state and the local parties are important to the encouragement, facilitation, and development of Geo-economic integration. On the other hand, other social struggles can easily happen during the production of cities. Therefore, these are also related to regional politics. When the economy is booming, since there is a lack of supply of infrastructure, housing, and other social services, societies will need to keep searching for new space for development among cities regions. China does not have much experience in regionalization. Particularly, this issue seldom appeared in tourism and hospitality literature. Therefore, this book enhances tourism literature by testing the tourism development-related issues of city integration in the Greater Bay Area. Furthermore, government or practitioners can improve the management of the city and tourism service using this book.

Chapter 1 is a general introduction of city integration in China and the Greater Bay Area within the global environment. Chapter 2 is a historical review, focusing on tourism development in Guangdong, Hong Kong, and Macau. Chapter 3 discusses the concept of city integration and the profile related to the Greater Bay Area. In Chapter 4, the impact of city integration on tourism development will be discussed. Chapter 5 describes the trends of city integration and tourism development. Chapter 6 investigates residents' attitude towards city integration and tourism development in the Greater Bay Area. Qualitative approach is designed and analysed using content analysis. This case study will provide a theoretical and practical perspective on city integration influence on tourism development in the Greater Bay Area.

Acknowledgements

We owe a substantial debt to several people and organizations for their comments and support throughout the writing of this book. Among all, special thanks to the Faculty of International Tourism and Management at the City University of Macau for providing the right intellectual environment for ensuring that this book was developed and completed, and also to The Chinese University of Hong Kong and Macau Foundation.

We deeply appreciate an impressive group of colleagues and friends, including but not limited to, Professor Kuai Peng Ip, Professor Hanqin Qiu, Professor Kevin Hannam, Professor Ivan Lai, Dr Ka Yin Chau, Dr Hong Chen, and Dr Iok Teng Kou, for their support, advice, and guidance. We are also grateful to our graduate students, Yulan Fan, Pengfei Shi, Xiaoshan He, and Hongyu Yu. Their help and contributions in maintaining the quality of this book are greatly appreciated. Without their support, this book would not have been possible.

Last, but by no means least, we would like to thank our families and partners for their encouragement and support. Reya Lam made a big difference – not least, all the hours of fun and enjoyment. Without them, we would not have been able to complete this book.

Jian Ming Luo
Chi Fung Lam
Hong Kong, China
December, 2019

1 An introduction to the Greater Bay Area in China

City development in China

The social and economic development of a city symbolizes and characterizes the country. Numerous opportunities in cities are available from various surrounding reform and development. These opportunities include historical traditions, natural environment, industrial features, and cultural resources (PWC, 2019). Urbanization, a remarkable social phenomenon since the nineteenth and twentieth century, transformed the configuration, regardless of spatial or social configuration, of human societies significantly (Luo, 2016). Powerful countries usually use mega-cities to symbolize the country. A typical mega-city is one big city surrounded by some, or many smaller cities, with efficient and integrated connections between cities. Urbanization is a great challenge to many academic researchers. The main issue is to understand cities in a more quantified method. In particular, how does a city begin? Why would city disappear? How should people measure a city or a metro area? There are many similar and contrasting arguments. All cities have their technical ends, and for good reasons. City planners need to know the effective area which their rules have effect on and which areas their services are aimed at (Berg, 2011).

The spatial distribution and evolution of cities characterize the urban function at the national level. The rapid expansion in the cities significantly affects the research of urban system in China. Since the beginning of the People's Republic of China in 1949, the urbanization in China has been ongoing in a very particular way. In 1949, the economy in China was purely planned economy, as were its urban conditions. This situation limited the possible policies available in 1978, when the economic reform began. The long-term goal of urbanization was to industrialize China. The immediate choice to improve the urban system was to optimize the economic structure and enhance infrastructure (Xu & Yeh, 2005) and hence there were no recognizable difference between cities with different sizes (Birch & Wachter, 2011).

One of the problems to study urbanization in China is the definition of urban population. This problem was particularly severe in 1983, when many counties were regrouped or reassigned into cities. Then, in 1984, many townships were reassigned into towns (Ma & Cui, 1987). In addition, the official record of urban population usually reported the total agricultural and non-agricultural population within the administrative boundaries of the cities, excluding counties under the jurisdiction of cities. Despite the above problems, the non-agricultural population is still a good proxy for the urbanization level in China, due to its robustness of the boundaries of cities and its involvements in urban activities (Ma & Cui, 1987; Luo, 2016; Luo & Lam, 2017).

Urbanization in China has increased rapidly since 1978. However, the increase of urbanization in 1978 was not caused by rural-urban migration. Some of the increase was caused by the increase in the designation of human settlement. Most of the increase was caused the 'city leading county' policy in 1979. This policy abolished many counties and combined these counties into one city (Yeh & Xu, 1990). Table 1.1 shows the number of cities in China increased from 194 to 1978 to over 600 in 2017.

Table 1.1 Divisions of administrative areas in China (1998–2017)

Year	Cities at prefecture level	Cities at county level	Total cities
2017	294	363	687
2016	293	360	653
2015	291	361	652
2014	288	361	649
2013	286	368	654
2012	285	368	653
2011	284	369	653
2010	283	370	653
2009	283	367	650
2008	283	368	651
2007	283	368	651
2006	283	369	652
2005	283	374	657
2004	283	374	657
2003	282	374	656
2002	282	374	656
2001	265	393	658
2000	259	400	659
1999	236	427	663
1998	227	437	664

Sources: National Bureau of Statistics of China, 2018.

According to recent forecasts by the United Nations (2010) and McKinsey Global Institute (2009), the), urban population in China will reach 1 billion in 2050 and it will have an annual growth rate of 20 million. Urbanization rate increased more than three times during the same period (Zhang, Luo, Xiao, & Guillet, 2013; Luo, Qiu, & Lam, 2016; Luo & Lam, 2016).

Before 1978, the Chinese government actively participated in the development of urban systems, through politics and public policies, which were the most crucial factors of urban system development in China. Politics and public policies did not only affect urban and city system development, but also population growth rate and distribution in the urban area (Yeh & Xu, 1990). However, the participation had gradually reduced since the open-door policy and economic reform in 1978. Population and resources were tightly controlled by the central government's public policies and ideologies before 1978. For example, the growth of large cities was reduced, while smaller towns were growing rapidly. Population in cities moved from the coastal areas to other more desirable locations, such as cities in the interior of China. These results cannot be easily or successfully achieved in other countries since these results require a huge amount of central control over human mobility and economic resources. These controls included the control of jobs, housing, and necessities, which are the main factors attracting people to move away from cities. The central ownership of industry provided such opportunities. After 1978, the allocation of resources was mainly determined by population and the production units' location and characteristics. Social areas were developed based on how these resources were allocated.

The aims and purposes of the growth of cities and metropolitan areas is to improve people's living standard and urban development (Yeh & Xu, 1984). The clustering of cities and towns has a long history in China (Yeh & Xu, 1984). China transformed the countries into 19 regions. Three regions were expected to become a world class cluster in 2020:

1   The Pearl River Delta (PRD), also known as the 'Factory of the World', specializes in advanced manufacturing. This region consists of Hong Kong, the world famous financial centre; Shenzhen, the 'Silicon Valley' in China,due to the number start-ups available, and the innovative products produced by these start-ups; Guangzhou, the manufacturing industry and logistic hub; and Macau and Zhuhia, the world leisure and tourism centre.

2   The Yangtze River Delta, driven by Shanghai, specializes in advanced manufacturing, technology, and innovation. It is also another gateway of the Asia-Pacific market.

3   The Beijing-Tianjin-Hebei region, driven by Beijing, is known as a political, educational, cultural, and R&D centre. Tianjin, with one of

the busiest ports in the world, is also known as the logistic centre of northern China. Hebei province is known for its heavy industries, including steel production.

Most of these urban clusters are located in the coastal region, which provides them with easy access to the world. Hence, these clusters were the first to boom and developed in the economic reform. As the development and economic reform continue, the Chinese government is moving the whole country up the value chain. The goal targets the three main clusters to become global innovation centres and smaller cities will focus on cleaner and more efficient industries, and therefore achieve sustainable and high-quality growth. The remaining 16 small or medium size cluster, which accounts for two to nine per cent of GDP in China, will aim at driving economic development at the provincial level (Preen, 2019).

A profile of the Greater Bay Area in China (GBA)

Ever since the economic reform and liberalization of China, China has become highly urbanized and accumulated enormous wealth. Guangdong–Hong Kong–Macau Greater Bay Area (GBA) is the latest urbanization initiative of China. As the name of the initiative suggests, the GBA comprises of Hong Kong and Macau, the two Special Administrative Regions in China, and nine cities in the Guangdong Province, which includes Guangzhou, Shenzhen, Zhuhai, Foshan, Huizhou, Dongguan, Zhongshan, Jiangmen, and Zhaoqing. This is also referred to as 9 + 2 cities plan. The total area of GBA is 56,000 km squared and the total population involved is over 70 million (around 5 per cent of the total population in China) (the Greater Bay Area, 2019) (see Figure 1.1).

The Greater Bay Area, due to its location and vast development of the PRD region, is of great importance to the Belt and Road Initiative. In addition, the transport system in The Greater Bay Area is highly developed. Since Hong Kong is an international maritime centre and Guangzhou and Shenzhen is one of the busiest ports in the world, the three cities, combined, become the most important aviation hub with a comprehensive transportation system.

The development of the Greater Bay Area is accorded the status of key strategic planning in the country's development blueprint, having great significance in the country's implementation of innovation-driven development and commitment to reform and opening-up. The goals include enhancing cooperation and integration between three important cities in The Greater Bay Area, Guangdong, Hong Kong, and Macau and to fully leverage the composite advantages and promote regional economic development. In

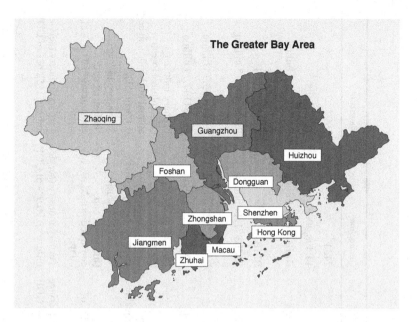

Figure 1.1 Map of Greater Bay Area.

addition, the blueprint also aims to develop it into an international first-class bay area for living, working, and travelling, with the main competitors being bay areas in San Francisco, New York, and Tokyo. The Greater Bay Area only occupies less than one per cent of land in China. However, around 12 per cent of China's GDP comes from this area. This area contributed US$1.5 trillion to China's GDP in 2017, which is two times more than the contribution of the bay area in San Francisco (Greater Bay Area, 2019).

Since the two SARs, Hong Kong and Macau, are operating under 'one country, two systems', the development of The Greater Bay Area will enrich this system and enhance the cooperation. This will not only provide enormous opportunities to people in Hong Kong and Macau, but also maintain prosperity and stability in the future. An additional objective was to conduct a supply-side restructuring, which aims at developing new economic drivers, and enhance the innovativeness and competitiveness of the Chinese economy. This will further deepen the reform and the opening up. In addition, a new system with international standard and a new platform with international cooperation will be developed. This will facilitate the development of the Belt and Road via 'two-way opening up', which develops the GBA into a supporting area, converging with the Silk Road Economic Belt and the twenty-first century Maritime Silk Road (Greater Bay Area, 2019) (see Table 1.2).

Table 1.2 Major social and economic indicators in GBA (2018)

	Hong Kong	Macao	Guangzhou	Shenzhen
Area (km^2)	1107	33	7434	1997
Population	7,482,500	667,400	14,498,000	12,528,000
Gross domestic product (GDP)	HK$2839.0 billion	MOP 440.10 billion	RMB2285.9 billion	RMB2422.2 billion
GDP per capita	HK$381,000	MOP 666,000	RMB155,000	RMB190,000
Value of total merchandise trade	HK$8232.9 billion	MOP 87.13 billion	RMB971.44 billion	RMB2801.15 billion
Value of export	HK$3875.9 billion	MOP 11.28 billion	RMB579.22 billion	RMB1653.36 billion
Value of import	HK$4357 billion	MOP 75.85 billion	RMB392.22 billion	RMB1147.79 billion
Industrial structure (% of GDP)	Primary industry (agriculture, forestry, animal husbandry, fishery): 0.1% of GDP	Primary industry (agriculture, forestry, animal husbandry, fishery): Not applicable	Primary industry (agriculture, forestry, animal husbandry, fishery): 1.1% of GDP	Primary industry (agriculture, forestry, animal husbandry, fishery): 0.1% of GDP
	Secondary Industry (industrial and construction): 7.5% of GDP	Secondary Industry (industrial and construction): 5.1% of GDP	Secondary Industry (industrial and construction): 28.0% of GDP	Secondary Industry (industrial and construction): 41.3% of GDP
	Tertiary industry (service industry): 92.4% of GDP	Tertiary industry (service industry): 94.9% of GDP	Tertiary industry (service industry): 70.9% of GDP	Tertiary industry (service industry): 58.6% of GDP

	Zhuhai	Foshan	Huizhou	Dongguan
Port cargo throughput	280 million tons	160,000 tons	590 million tons	240 million tons
Passenger throughput	Visitor Arrivals to Hong Kong: 65.1 million passenger trips; Hong Kong International Airport: 74.7 million passenger trips	Visitors received: 32.611 million passenger trips; Macao International Airport: 71.66 million passenger trips	Visitors received: 62.756 million passenger trips; Guangzhou Baiyuan International Airport: 65.84 million passenger trips	Overnight visitors received: 60.22 million passenger trips; Shenzhen Bao'an International Airport: 45.61 million passenger trips
Area (km^2)	1736	3798	11,347	2460
Population	1,766,000	7,657,000	4,777,000	8,343,000
Gross domestic product (GDP)	RMB291.5 billion	RMB993.6 billion	RMB410.3 billion	RMB827.9 billion
GDP per capita	RMB159,000	RMB128,000	RMB85,000	RMB99,000
Value of total merchandise trade	RMB299.01 billion	RMB435.74 billion	RMB341.6 billion	RMB1226.44 billion
Value of export	RMB188.30 billion	RMB315.36 billion	RMB233.31 billion	RMB702.74 billion
Value of import	RMB110.71 billion	RMB120.38 billion	RMB118.29 billion	RMB523.70 billion

continued

Table 1.2 Continued

	Zhuhai	Foshan	Huizhou	Dongguan
Industrial structure (% of GDP)	Primary industry (agriculture, forestry, animal husbandry, fishery): 1.8% of GDP	Primary industry (agriculture, forestry, animal husbandry, fishery): 1.5% of GDP	Primary industry (agriculture, forestry, animal husbandry, fishery): 4.5% of GDP	Primary industry (agriculture, forestry, animal husbandry, fishery): 0.3% of GDP
	Secondary Industry (industrial and construction): 50.2% of GDP	Secondary Industry (industrial and construction): 58.4% of GDP	Secondary Industry (industrial and construction): 54.8% of GDP	Secondary Industry (industrial and construction): 47.4% of GDP
	Tertiary industry (service industry): 48% of GDP	Tertiary industry (service industry): 40.1% of GDP	Tertiary industry (service industry): 40.7% of GDP	Tertiary industry (service industry): 52.3% of GDP
Port cargo throughput	136 million tons	79.674 million tons	72.11 million tons	160 million tons
Passenger throughput	Visitors received: 39.807 million passenger trips	Visitors received: 49.29 million passenger trips	Visitors received: 539.36 million passenger trips	Visitors received: 414.19 million passenger trips
	Zhuhai Jinwan International Airport: 9.217 million passenger trips	Foshan Shadi Airport: 470,000 passenger trips	Huizhou Pingtan Airport: 957,000 passenger trips	

	Zhongshan	Jiangmen	Zhaoqing
Area (km^2)	1784	9507	14,891
Population	3,260,000	4,562,000	4,115,000
Gross domestic product (GDP)	RMB363.3 billion	RMB290.0 billion	RMB220.2 billion
GDP per capita	RMB111,000	RMB63,000	RMB53,000
Value of total merchandise trade	RMB258.15 billion	RMB138.52 billion	RMB35.79 billion
Value of export	RMB205.56 billion	RMB107.56 billion	RMB22.23 billion
Value of import	RMB52.59 billion	RMB30.96 billion	RMB13.56 billion
Industrial structure (% of GDP)	Primary industry (agriculture, forestry, animal husbandry, fishery): 1.9% of GDP	Primary industry (agriculture, forestry, animal husbandry, fishery): 7.2% of GDP	Primary industry (agriculture, forestry, animal husbandry, fishery): 14.8% of GDP
	Secondary Industry (industrial and construction): 50.3% of GDP	Secondary Industry (industrial and construction): 48.1% of GDP	Secondary Industry (industrial and construction): 46.9% of GDP
	Tertiary industry (service industry): 47.8% of GDP	Tertiary industry (service industry): 44.7% of GDP	Tertiary industry (service industry): 38.3% of GDP
Port cargo throughput	80.44 million tons	82.67 million tons	39.31 million tons
Passenger throughput	Visitors received: 133.35 million passenger trips	Visitors received: 22.59 million passenger trips	Visitors received: 42.19 million passenger trips

- Hong Kong

  Hong Kong is located on the coast of China and is the heart of Asia. This huge geographic advantage makes Hong Kong the perfect location for connecting China with many key Asian markets, and the rest of the world. According to The United States' Heritage Foundation and the Fraser Institute in Canada, Hong Kong was ranked the freest city in the world 24 years consecutively (Fraser Institute, 2017). The International Institute for Management Development World Competitiveness (IMD, 2018) also ranked Hong Kong as one of the most competitive economies in the world. Hong Kong has consistently been one of the top five easiest places to conduct business (World Bank, 2019). In addition, Hong Kong was the seventh largest trading entity in 2017 (World Trade Organization, 2018).

- Macau

  Macau, a city located in the south of Guangdong and a part of the PRD region, consist of three parts, Macau Peninsula, Taipa, and Coloane. Macau also connects with China via Zhuhai. The Macao Peninsula is at the centre of Macau. Taipa and Coloane were two separated islands and were connected via land reclamation, which eventually were developed into Cotai. Today, Cotai contains numerous resorts and hotels. Macau pursues an open economic policy with the lowest tax rate in the region and a sound fiscal system. There is no restriction on foreign exchange. It is a free port and has its own customs territory. Macao is an economy with strong economic vitality in the Asia-Pacific region. Hence, it is another link connecting China and the rest of the world. Macau's economy was traditionally concentrated on tourism and the gambling industry. Over 45 per cent of the industrial structure in Macau comes from the gambling and junket activities. Despite the ranking of Macau not being as high as Hong Kong in the eyes of the Heritage Foundation in the United States, Macau was ranked the thirty-second freest country in the world for almost a decade.

- Guangzhou

  Guangzhou, the capital of Guangdong, is in the southern part of China. Guangzhou contains three advanced manufacturing pillar industries, which are automobiles, electronics, and petrochemical. These are the engines of Guangzhou's development and are supported by six cutting-edge production bases, which are automobiles, ship and marine engineering equipment, nuclear power equipment, computer numerical control equipment, petrochemicals and fine steel manufacturing. There are also more than 50 industrial areas and parks, focusing on automobiles, petrochemicals and electronics in the east, port-related equipment manufacturing in the south, and airport-based economy in the north. Guangzhou is located near the Pearl River port, which is an excellent port to access the world. In addition, the great railway transportation system in Guangzhou further connects Guangzhou to the rest of China. Guangzhou South Railway Station, a station that can serve 100 million passengers, is a comprehensive transport hub serving Southern Guangdong. There are five high-speed railways (Wuhan–Guangzhou High-speed Railway, Guangzhou–Shenzhen–Hong Kong Express Rail Link, Guiyang–Guangzhou High-speed Railway, Nanning–Guangzhou High-speed Railway and Guangzhou–Zhuhai Intercity Railway) and two metro lines. Guangzhou–Foshan Circular and Foshan–Dongguan Intercity Railways are under construction.

• Shenzhen

Shenzhen, also known as 'Pengcheng' (the City of Giant Eagle), is located on the coast of South China. It is also connected directly to the New Territories of Hong Kong. It is one of few cities (which are called Special Economic Zones) that was reformed and opened to the world under the Open Door Policy in 1980s. In March 1981, Shenzhen was promoted to a sub-provincial city. Ten years later, Shenzhen received legislative power over its special economic zone from the central government. The transportation system in Shenzhen, including Beijing-Kowloon Through Train, Guangzhou-Shenzhen-Hong Kong Express Rail Link and Xiamen-Shenzhen Railway, is efficient and convenient. Shenzhen has developed a convenient and efficient integrated transport system. Beijing-Kowloon Through Train, Guangzhou-Shenzhen-Hong Kong Express Rail Link and Xiamen–Shenzhen railway form a national railway node at Shenzhen. There are eight lines in Shenzhen Metro. One of the most important line is the Longhua Line, which connects the mass transit railway in Hong Kong. This well-developed transportation system allows people and goods to transfer to other cities in Pearl River Delta. Shenzhen Bao'an International Airport is connected to 145 cities in 17 countries/regions with 190 passenger air routes and 34 freight routes. Shenzhen has boundary checkpoints covering land, sea, and air travel. It is the city with the largest number of checkpoints, largest inbound/outbound passenger flow and vehicular flow in China. There are four pillar industries and seven emerging industries in Shenzhen. The four pillar industries are advanced technology, modern logistics, financial services and cultural industry, and the seven emerging industries are biotechnology, Internet, new energy, new materials, cultural and creative industries, new generation information technology, as well as energy conservation and environmental protection, plus future industries on life and health, marine, aerospace and aviation, robots, wearable devices, and smart equipment.

- Zhuhai

Zhuhai, another Special Economic Zone developed in the 1980s, is located at the south-central part of Guangdong Province. More specifically, it is located on the north of Macau and South of Zhongshan. Zhuhai has been developing rapidly since the Open Door Policy. There are six basic industries in Zhuhai, which are electronic information, home appliances, electricity and energy, biopharmaceuticals and medical devices, petrochemicals and precision machinery. There are two emerging industries in Zhuhai, which are printing supplies and yacht manufacturing. Similar to Shenzhen, Zhuhai has convenient land, sea, and air transport. Zhuhai Port is one of the main coastal ports of the country and is one of the five major ports in Guangdong Province.

- Foshan

Foshan is located on the east of Guangzhou, which is also the south-central part of Guangdong. The travelling time between Foshan and Hong Kong or Macao is about two hours. The transportation network of Foshan is good. Modern transportation methods, such as air, railway, highway, and marine, are all available in Foshan. There are flights connecting Foshan Airport to cities such as Beijing, Shanghai, and Shijiazhuang. Foshan is building a new airport and is expected to commence in 2020 (CAPA, 2018). The new airport will be one of the main airports in Guangdong. It will be able to process about 50 million passengers. Also, the Guangzhou-Foshan Line is the first railway in the country which connects across cities, including Guangzhou, Zhongshan, Zhuhai, Hong Kong, and Macau. Foshan is a manufacturing-based city. The main industries are machinery equipment, household appliances, ceramic building materials, metal processing and metal products, textiles and garments, electronic information, food and beverages, fine chemicals and pharmaceuticals, household goods, etc., as well as emerging industries including optoelectronics, environmental protection, new materials, new medicines, and new energy vehicles. As both city and country become more developed, Foshan is the first city that has attempted agricultural industrialisation, focusing on horticulture, aquaculture, and animal husbandry. So far, this has been very successful. Foshan has the largest plantation base of phalaenopsis in the country and the largest plantation base of high-quality lilies in the province. Consequently, Foshan is well-known as 'home of eels in China', 'home of freshwater fish fry in China', and 'home of flowers and trees in China'.

- Huizhou

Huizhou, the 'gateway of Eastern Guangdong' and the second largest city in the GBA, is located in the southeast of Guangdong. The excellent environment and rich tourism resources makes it an excellent tourist destination. The natural environment in Huizhou is extraordinary. Over 60 per cent of the land in Huizhou is covered by forest. Huizhou has one of the best air qualities in China. Its green development index has ranked the first in the Guangdong Province. Huizhou is rich in mineral resources. Over 30 different types of minerals, such as iron, coal tungsten, and titanium, can be found in Huizhou. The abundance of land also makes Huizhou an ideal place for agricultural goods, such as rice, sugarcane, peanuts, lychees, etc. Besides agricultural products, Huizhou also produces aquatic products, such as high-quality salts. Over 800 types of aquatic goods are produced in Huizhou. Local specialties, including 'mei cai' (dried pickled vegetables), glutinous rice wine, tangerines, chickens, herbal oils, calamari, abalones, 'South China Sea pearl', and bamboo shoots are popular. The 'two ports, three networks' programme is the next central transportation infrastructure development in Huizhou. The goal is to develop a modern comprehensive transportation network in Huizhou. The Xiamen-Shenzhen railways along with the two railway stations, Huizhou South and Huidong Railway Station, was opened in 2013. There are two pillar industries in Huizhou, electronic information and petrochemicals. Together with automotive and equipment manufacturing, as well as clean energy industries, these industries form the modern industrial system of Huizhou. The Daya Bay Petrochemical Zone can produce over 20 million tons of oil and 2.2 million tons of ethylene per year, which makes it the most productive petrochemical zone in the country. The Huizhou Zhongkai Hi-tech Industrial Development Zone is the country's first national electronic information industrial base, with a complete supply chain of mobile communications, panel display, automotive electronics, LED, and new energy. Huizhou is the country's production base for women's shoes and is famous for menswear.

- Dongguan

  Dongguan is located at the south-central part of Guangdong Province, on the east bank of the Pearl River Estuary and sits in the centre of the Guangdong–Hong Kong–Macao Greater Bay Area, as well as the middle section of the Guangzhou-Shenzhen science and technology innovation corridor. Dongguan is connected to an extensive network of expressways, including Guangzhou-Shenzhen, Dongguan-Shenzhen, Guangzhou-Shenzhen Yanjiang, Boluo-Shen, Conghua-Dongguan, Chaozhou-Dongguan expressways, and Humen Bridge. In terms of railways, Dongguan is located at the junction of Beijing-Kowloon, Guangzhou-Meizhou-Shantou, Guangzhou-Shenzhen, and Guangzhou-Kowloon Railways. It is very convenient to travel to and from Hong Kong, Macao, Beijing, Shanghai, and eastern China. Currently, there are three intercity railways under construction, namely Guangzhou-Dongguan-Shenzhen intercity railway, Dongguan-Huizhou intercity railway and Foshan-Dongguan intercity railway, which will be connecting the city centres of Guangzhou, Shenzhen, and Huizhou. There is also Humen Port. Dongguan's pillar industries are electronic information, electrical machinery and equipment; textiles, garments, shoes and accessories; food and beverage processing, and papermaking and paper products. It has also formed a cluster of emerging industries including LED lighting, new flat display, and photovoltaics.

- Zhongshan

  Since Zhongshan is located in the south-central part of PRD, it connects Guangzhou, Hong Kong, and Macau naturally. This also makes Zhongshan an important transportation node in PRD. Zhongshan is the only city in Guangdong which owns a bonded logistics centre. Zhongshan is famous for its advanced manufacturing and modern service industry since it is one of the pilot cities for industrial upgrade. The pillar industries in Zhongshan are equipment manufacturing, household appliances, textiles and garments, electronics, lighting, healthcare and pharmaceuticals, furniture, small home appliances and hardware products, as well as emerging industries, such as the modern service industry and yacht industry. The port-area equipment manufacturing base hosts many large-scale state-owned enterprises, such as China Shipbuilding Industry Corporation, China Railway Group Limited, China National Offshore Oil Corporation, and Sinoconst Steel Structure Co. Ltd.

- Jiangmen

  Jiangmen is located on the east of Zhongshan Zhuhai and the west of Guangzhou and Foshan, located at the west of PRD. It is not too far away from Hong Kong and Macau. There are eight expressways connecting Jiangmen with other places, namely Foshan-Kaiping, Kaiping-Yangjiang, Xinhui-Taishan, Jiangmen-Heshan, Zhongshan-Jiangmen, Jiangmen-Zhuhai, Jiangmen-Zhaoqing, and the western costal expressways. With the Guangzhou-Zhuhai intercity railway opened in 2011, Jiangmen was incorporated into the 'one-hour economic circle' of the PRD. Jiangmen has two ports, Xinhui Port and Taishan Guanghai Port, that achieved the national class 1 cargo port standard. Yinzhouhu waters can accommodate vessels of over 10,000 tons. The emerging industries in Jiangmen, such as new energy, new lighting, new materials, high-end equipment manufacturing, and green household appliances are developing rapidly. The pillar industries in Jiangmen include motorcycles and auto parts manufacturing, textiles and garments, papermaking, shipbuilding, food, packaging materials, bathroom accessories and sanitary hardware, printing, and electro-mechanics. Jiangmen is an important supplier of agricultural products and by-products for the PRD, Hong Kong, and Macao. It is the first agricultural cooperation pilot zone with Taiwan in the Guangdong province.

- Zhaoqing

Zhaoqing, also known as 'home of gold' of Guangdong, is located at the west of Foshan and the north of Jiangmen, which makes it located at the central-western part of Guangdong Zhaoqing is the largest city, measured in terms of land size, in the GBA. It has eight ports with well-developed transportation network. Zhaoqing New Port is one important ports of China. There are three expressways, 321, 324, and Guangzhou-Foshan-Zhaoqing, connecting Zhaoqing to the rest of the country. In addition, the Pearl River Delta Ring Road, Shantou-Kunming, and Shantou-Zhanjiang expressways further improve the efficiency of the transportation system. On top of the above-mentioned expressways, Nanning-Guangzhou and Shantou-Zhangjiang high-speed railway allows passengers to reach to the Zhaoqing New District directly, while the Guangzhou-Foshan-Zhaoqing intercity railway allows passengers to reach the city centre directly. The pillar industries in Zhaoqing include new energy vehicles industry, advanced equipment manufacturing, energy conservation and environmental protection, high-end new electronic information and biomedicine. In addition, Zhaoqing is developing three industrial clusters with value above 100 billion RMB for the pillar industries. Zhaoqing is also famous for its gold mines, which are mainly concentrated at Gaoyao District, Huaiji County, and Fengkai County. While the mines in

Zhaoqing contains limestone for cement, limestone for flux, gypsum, granite for overcoating, granite for construction, porcelain clay, inkstone, mineral water, geothermal water, andinkstone, particularly 'duanyan' which one type of inkstone, is of particular importance. Other than 'home of gold', Zhaoqing is also called 'capital of inkstone in China'. The mountains and historical scenic spots in Zhaoqing are splendid. For example, Xinghu Lake Scenic Area, is one of the national key scenic spots; Fengkai Lungshan Scenic Area and Huaiji Yanyan Scenic Area, which are two provincial-level scenic spots; and Dinghu Mountain, which is one of the 'four famous mountains in Guangdong' and is home to the first nature reserve in China listed by UNESCO as an international biosphere reserve.

Summary

This chapter introduces the Greater Bay Area in China. The National Development and Reform Commission, and the governments of Guangdong, Hong Kong, and Macao signed the Framework Agreement on Deepening Guangdong–Hong Kong–Macao Cooperation in the Development of the Greater Bay Area in Hong Kong by 2017. The Framework Agreement sets the goals and principles of cooperation and establishes the key cooperation areas in the development of the Greater Bay Area. Since then, the relevant Central Government departments and the three governments have strived for policy breakthroughs with an innovative and open mind in taking forward the development of the Greater Bay Area jointly. It is the hope of the remaining chapters will provide you a broader understanding of city development in the Greater Bay Area in China.

References

Berg, Nate (2011). *Defining Cities in a Metropolitan World.* Received on 11 January 2019 from www.citylab.com/design/2011/09/defining-cities-metropolitan-world/102/

Birch, E. L., & Wachter, S. M. (2011). *Global Urbanization.* Philadelphia, PA: University of Pennsylvania Press.

CAPA (2018). New Foshan Airport. [Online]. Retrieved 1 February 2020, from https://centreforaviation.com/data/profiles/newairports/new-foshan-airport

Fraser Institute (2017). Economic Freedom of the World: 2017 Annual Report. [Online]. Retrieved 1 December 2019, from www.fraserinstitute.org/studies/economic-freedom-of-the-world-2017-annual-report

Greater Bay Area (2019). *Outline Development Plan for the Guangdong–Hong Kong–Macao Greater Bay Area.* Received on 11 August 2019, from www.bayarea.gov.hk/en/outline/plan.html

IMD (2018). IMD World Competitiveness Rankings 2018. [Online]. Retrieved 1 December 2019, from www.imd.org/wcc/world-competitiveness-center-rankings/world-competitiveness-ranking-2018/

Luo, J. M. (2016). *Urbanization and tourism development in China.* New York: Nova Science Publishers, Incorporated.

Luo, J. M., & Lam, C. F. (2016). A qualitative study of urbanization effects on hotel development. *Journal of Hospitality and Tourism Management*, 29, 135–142.

Luo, J. M., & Lam, C. F. (2017). Urbanization effects on hotel performance: A case study in China. *Cogent Business & Management*, 4(1), 1412873.

Luo, J. M., Qiu, H., & Lam, C. F. (2016). Urbanization impacts on regional tourism development: a case study in China. *Current Issues in Tourism*, 19(3), 282–295.

Ma Laurence, J. C., & Cui, G. (1987). Administrative changes and urban population in China. *Annals of the Association of American Geographers*, 77(3), 373–395.

McKinsey Global Institute (2009). Preparing for China's Urban Billion. [Online]. Retrieved 1 February 2020, from www.mckinsey.com/insights/urbanization/preparing_for_urban_billion_in_china

Preen, M. (2019). *China city-clusters policy: clusters to boost regional development.* Received on 12 August 2019 from www.clustercollaboration.eu/news/china-city-clusters-policy-clusters-boost-regional-development

PWC (2019). *Chinese cities of opportunity 2018.* Received on 11 January 2019 from www.pwccn.com/en/research-and-insights/chinese-cities-of-opportunities-2018-report.html

United Nations (UN). (2010). *World Urbanization Prospects: The 2009 Revision*, United Nations, Department of Economic and Social Affairs, Population Division, New York.

Work Bank (2019). Doing Business 2019. [Online]. Retrieved 21 December 2019, from www.doingbusiness.org/content/dam/doingBusiness/media/Annual-Reports/English/DB2019-report_web-version.pdf

World Trade Organization (2018). World Trade Statistical Review 2018. [Online]. Retrieved 21 December 2019, from www.wto.org/english/res_e/statis_e/wts2018_e/wts2018_e.pdf

Xu, J., & Yeh, A. G. (2005). City repositioning and competitiveness building in regional development: new development strategies in Guangzhou, China. *International Journal of Urban and Regional Research*, 29(2), 283–308.

Yeh, A. G. O., & Xu, X. (1984). Provincial variation of urbanization and urban primacy in China. *The Annals of Regional Science*, 18(3), 1–20.

Yeh, A. G. O., & Xu, X. (1990). New cities and city system development in China. *Asian Geographer*, 9, 11–38.

Zhang, H. Q., Luo, J. M., Xiao, Q., & Guillet, B. D. (2013). The impact of urbanization on hotel development: Evidence from Guangdong Province in China. *International Journal of Hospitality Management*, 34, 92–98.

2 History of tourism development in the Greater Bay Area

Hong Kong: Asian destinations

Hong Kong, also known as the Hong Kong Special Administrative Region (HKSAR), is located on the east of the Pearl River Delta Region (PRD). With a population of over 7 million people in around $1000\,km^2$, Hong Kong is one of the most densely populated areas (GovHK, 2019). Hong Kong, Kowloon, and the New Territories became a colony of the British Empire in 1842 (The First Opium War), 1860 (The Second Opium War), and 1898, respectively. All three territories returned to the rule of China in 1997. Ever since the reunification, Hong Kong has been operating under 'one country, two systems', which allows a high degree of autonomy in executive, legislative, and judicial aspects. Since Hong Kong is located on the Southeast coast of China with easy access to many major cities in China, Hong Kong naturally becomes a gateway to mainland China for international business through its world-class internationally recognized container ports, airport, and telecommunication networks. The 'one country, two systems' also provides an internationally recognized common law system and an independent judiciary for legal services (HKTDC, 2019). Given its geographic location convenience, rich historical back-ground, relatively low crime rate, and political stability, Hong Kong excels in many areas, such as commercial ports (ranked tenth in the world), tourism (ranked fourth in the world), and finance (ranked third in the world) (UNWTO, 2018; Yen, 2017, 2019).

Despite its geographic location and rich history, the success of Hong Kong, especially tourism, is not without reasons. Both British and China government emphasize the importance of tourism in Hong Kong. Hong Kong began its development as a small fishing and farming village, and later became a manufacturing centre under governance of the British Empire, Hong Kong then experienced a shift of manufacturing to China in the 1980s. Hong Kong began to focus more on tertiary industries, such as tourism, with the aim for it to become the main business centre in Asia. The government begins by establishing the Hong Kong Tourism Association (HKTA), which was renamed as the Hong Kong Tourism Board (HKTB) in 2001 (Choi, 2007). The purpose of the Hong Kong Tourism Board is to 'market and promote Hong Kong as a travel destination worldwide and to enhance visitors' experience' (HKTB, 2019a). The contribution of tourism to the Hong Kong GDP reached 3.6 per cent in 1990. Hong Kong's tourism was ranked eighteenth in the same year (Hong Kong Economy, 2005). Eventually, the ranking of Hong Kong tourism reached twelfth and provided around four per cent of employment in 2003. The Financial Secretary officially listed tourism as the 'four pillars' of Hong Kong's economy in 2003. More recently, the ranking of Hong Kong tourism reached fourth in 2018 based on the number of international tourists' arrival (UNWTO, 2018). As a small territory, Hong Kong attracts tourists from more than 200 countries (Census and Statistics Department, 2018). Table 2.1 shows the number of tourist arrivals from 1988 to 2017.

The success of Hong Kong's tourism is not without trouble. As shown in Table 2.1, the total tourist arrival experiences several slumps. For example, the outbreak of severe acute respiratory syndrome (SARS) in 2003, the 2008 financial crisis, anti-parallel trading protest in 2012, Occupy Central in 2014, the tightening of visa policy from China to Hong Kong in 2015, Mong Kok Riot in 2016. Of course, HKTB and the Hong Kong government responded proactively. For example, in 2004, HKTB introduced *A Symphony of Lights*, a lighting and music show that used harbour-front buildings between Central and Wan Chai to tell the story of Hong Kong; and Avenue of Stars, an attraction designated to cater for visitors' interest in Hong Kong movies, which honours the contribution of the industry's leading actors/actresses (HKTB, 2005). *A Symphony of Lights* also achieved a Guinness World Record for, 'The world's Largest Permanent Light and Sound Show'. In 2005, Disneyland Hong Kong was opened in Lantau Island and it is the second theme park, other than Ocean Park, in Hong Kong (HKTB, 2005). In 2006, HKTB initiated the Cultural & Heritage Celebration, an event that combines four major local festivals, the Birthday of Tin Hau, the Lord Buddha and Tam Kung, and the Cheung Chau Jiao Festival. The Cheung Chau Jiao Festival is eventually inscribed onto the third national list of intangible cultural heritage (HK Government News, 2011). To develop cruise tourism, the Hong Kong government established the Advisory Committee on the Cruise Industry (ACCI) in 2008 and developed a new cruise terminal at the former runway of the previous HK Airport in Kai Tak (HKTB, 2007).

One of the most important and influential measures that indicate tourist arrival slumps is the Individual Visit Scheme. Before the Individual Visit

Table 2.1 Tourist Arrival Number in Hong Kong (1988–2017)

Year	Tourist arrival	China	The Americans			Europe				Middle Eas
			United States of America	Canada	South and Central America	United Kingdom	Germany	France	Italy	South Afric
1988	6,167,221	683,604	749,244	166,024	36,830	285,590	123,737	98,174	70,582	22,147
1989	5,984,501	730,408	624,400	150,509	38,011	269,716	118,919	82,561	59,515	20,524
1990	6,580,850	754,376	612,262	155,695	39,735	279,333	118,556	83,272	63,855	21,795
1991	6,795,413	875,062	619,685	161,784	40,928	275,626	136,967	96,044	69,959	24,039
1992	8,010,524	1,149,002	694,290	180,231	49,732	314,231	172,200	128,497	80,634	25,556
1993	8,937,500	1,732,978	755,666	189,432	63,215	339,162	219,706	138,569	76,289	33,610
1994	9,331,156	1,943,678	776,039	185,290	65,080	379,577	236,384	138,920	82,341	34,662
1995	10,199,994	2,243,245	748,911	174,656	62,775	360,545	249,266	129,676	75,766	32,983
1996	1,1702,735	2,311,184	751,275	165,887	55,970	397,153	275,892	126,896	67,891	30,324
1997	10,406,261	2,297,128	800,539	178,046	65,202	340,263	235,006	133,807	67,065	26,500
1998	9,574,711	2,597,442	773,309	194,351	61,745	325,738	170,716	115,543	63,216	23,830
1999	10,678,460	3,083,859	802,705	210,899	64,179	308,754	172,166	122,811	64,792	24,756
2000	13,059,477	3,784,845	966,008	253,095	76,805	367,938	193,837	142,487	70,743	30,908
2001	13,725,332	4,448,583	935,717	249,707	73,143	360,581	173,359	136,876	65,753	32,504
2002	16,566,382	6,825,199	1,000,844	26,497	81,029	379,965	172,654	146,714	71,969	30,783
2003	15,536,839	8,467,211	683,791	186,809	55,307	281,318	116,966	95,844	50,756	29,278
2004	21,810,630	12,245,862	1,051,696	273,925	73,951	411,287	169,661	148,131	79,016	54,371
2005	23,259,417	12,541,400	1,143,089	308,842	113,419	464,601	204,625	185,601	97,926	77,520
2006	25,251,124	13,591,342	1,159,025	335,697	135,915	516,495	213,837	200,820	108,374	76,820
2007	28,169,293	15,484,789	1,230,927	395,167	157,515	601,168	234,763	231,091	118,841	72,897
2008	29,506,616	16,862,003	1,146,364	379,046	159,324	563,984	224,665	229,349	110,583	65,024
2009	29,590,000	17,957,000	1,070,000	362,000	136,000	514,000	211,000	218,000	103,000	62,000
2010	36,030,331	22,684,000	1,171,000	404,000	174,000	516,000	230,000	240,000	119,000	78,000
2011	41,921,310	28,100,000	1,212,000	411,000	198,000	507,000	224,000	234,000	117,000	80,000
2012	48,620,000	34,911,000	1,150,000	393,000	201,000	533,000	223,000	226,000	116,000	71,000
2013	54,298,804	40,745,000	1,110,000	354,000	202,000	513,000	221,000	228,000	113,000	68,000
2014	60,838,836	47,248,000	1,131,000	354,000	194,000	521,000	219,000	217,000	112,000	71,000
2015	59,307,596	45,842,000	1,181,000	358,000	189,000	530,000	214,000	210,000	108,000	71,000
2016	56,654,903	42,778,000	1,212,000	369,000	192,000	552,000	227,000	214,000	105,000	66,000
2017	58,472,157	44,445,000	1,216,000	370,000	196,000	555,000	225,000	204,000	105,000	65,000
Correlation	Before 2003	0.963802853	0.913519922	−0.1125	0.91449521	0.7999	0.439051	0.79507	0.07275	0.6305127
	After 2003	0.998398354	0.336974154	0.33321	0.840578879	0.341564	0.407375	0.32666	0.33491	0.0065353

Sources: Hong Kong Tourism Board, 1989–2018.

Scheme, people from Mainland China could only visit Hong Kong or Macau via group tours. With the introduction of the Individual Visit Scheme, tourists from Mainland China could travel to Hong Kong in their individual capacity. The Individual Visit Scheme was first introduced in Dongguan, Zhongshan, Jiangmen, and Foshan in 2003 (Commerce and Economic Development Bureau (CEDB), 2019), and was expanded to the entire Guangdong Province and many other cities in China. Table 2.2 shows the effective date of implementation and the cities in China which join the Scheme. Initially, the Scheme was a measure to respond to the SARS outbreak in Hong Kong by increasing the number visitors to Hong Kong (Education Bureau, 2019). After the introduction of the Scheme, tourist arrival experienced a dramatic increase in 2004 to 21.81 million. Tourist

	Oceania		North Asia		South and South East Asia						
ddle East	Australia	New Zealand	Japan	South Korea	Indonesia	Malaysia	Philippines	Singapore	Thailand	India	Taiwan
8,261	259,163	43,639	1,240,470	101,362	106,498	126,741	158,712	187,450	187,955	78,476	1,094,004
5,988	259,025	43,061	1,176,189	166,995	79,543	118,963	162,135	165,613	175,546	76,065	1,132,904
6,813	255,294	45,456	1,331,677	184,744	106,599	155,843	170,896	200,871	213,868	78,488	1,344,641
9,338	235,064	42,355	1,259,837	184,592	126,328	211,569	183,523	229,394	253,502	76,463	1,298,039
6,338	261,182	42,873	1,324,399	196,282	160,896	232,910	229,567	283,229	319,663	80,022	1,640,032
1,081	264,722	47,830	1,280,905	225,078	174,346	234,127	236,363	289,717	293,495	78,911	1,777,310
9,113	267,158	49,180	1,440,632	282,392	176,014	202,181	249,698	270,585	285,041	80,099	1,665,330
5,176	280,080	50,130	1,691,283	352,981	184,417	222,319	295,018	279,514	265,844	86,151	1,761,111
5,932	310,597	58,038	2,382,890	396,549	174,960	263,670	376,746	349,768	262,735	105,838	1,821,279
1,328	293,974	52,786	1,368,988	357,538	174,947	269,337	326,418	339,689	214,782	89,320	1,782,580
7,351	272,454	54,135	945,334	179,499	104,885	235,928	214,556	331,610	130,405	93,048	1,812,634
0,838	281,151	47,481	1,020,307	259,549	188,069	262,940	259,858	351,175	176,417	103,114	2,000,180
1,108	352,409	58,185	1,382,417	372,639	236,275	314,857	278,460	450,569	228,774	131,368	2,385,739
4,352	324,156	57,501	1,336,538	425,732	212,260	286,338	293,105	421,166	241,480	161,752	2,418,827
7,337	343,294	61,887	1,395,020	457,438	223,590	318,854	329,604	426,166	259,336	193,705	2,428,776
6,636	254,254	48,490	867,160	368,176	164,101	208,686	234,260	265,729	185,398	178,130	1,852,378
1,030	408,940	71,742	1,126,250	539,190	232,311	339,709	336,673	463,920	316,910	244,364	2,074,795
0,822	525,577	89,522	1,210,848	642,480	260,487	392,047	391,049	573,330	380,412	273,487	2,130,565
0,110	563,933	97,797	1,311,111	718,758	323,987	445,993	454,036	588,474	395,532	294,079	2,177,232
5,681	633,599	117,215	1,324,336	876,231	366,217	504,487	552,942	631,963	387,219	317,510	2,238,731
1,971	643,538	113,984	1,324,797	904,320	348,938	490,561	568,540	632,637	403,301	350,674	2,240,481
5,000	600,000	102,000	1,204,000	619,000	354,000	442,000	564,000	624,000	388,000	367,000	2,010,000
2,000	651,000	108,000	1,317,000	891,000	453,000	579,000	603,000	710,000	450,000	531,000	2,165,000
9,000	645,000	103,000	1,284,000	1,021,000	521,000	633,000	660,000	794,000	480,000	498,000	2,149,000
6,000	632,000	98,000	1,255,000	1,078,000	512,000	625,000	710,000	728,000	502,000	414,000	2,089,000
1,000	610,000	98,000	1,057,000	1,084,000	517,000	649,000	705,000	700,000	535,000	435,000	2,100,000
9,000	604,000	101,000	1,079,000	1,251,000	492,000	590,000	635,000	738,000	485,000	516,000	2,032,000
0,000	574,000	96,000	1,049,000	1,243,000	414,000	54,500	704,000	675,000	529,000	532,000	2,016,000
6,000	576,000	97,000	1,092,000	1,392,000	464,000	536,000	791,000	674,000	595,000	481,000	2,011,000
0,000	568,000	107,000	1,230,000	1,488,000	482,000	517,000	894,000	628,000	560,000	393,000	2,011,000
11677676	0.915689	0.923871894	0.266247	0.912302152	0.860603	0.896566	0.81589888	0.9341775	0.175216	0.91093	0.949048
34563419	0.280052	0.141598829	−0.58581	0.928999072	0.812501	0.123456	0.86505034	0.6222347	0.923483	0.76944	−0.61357

arrival continues to increase until 2014, even during 2008 Financial Crisis. As shown in the Table 2.1 historically, the correlation between total tourist arrival and tourist arrival from China is extremely high. Before 2003, the correlation between total tourist arrival and individual country tourist arrival are quite high. However, after 2003, not only the correlation between China and total tourist arrival increases, the correlation between countries other than China and total tourist arrival decrease dramatically (with a few exceptions, such as Canada, South Korea, Philippines, and Thailand).

The Individual Visit Scheme brings both benefits and costs. The benefits include the economic revenue, tax revenue, employment, etc., which is generated by the increase of visitors (see Table 2.2). In addition, since more tourists will encourage investors to invest in more infrastructures,

Table 2.2 Individual visit scheme implementation date and cities involved

Effective date	Cities/provinces
July 2003	Dongguan, Foshan, Zhongshan, Jiangmen
August 2003	Guangzhou, Shenzhen, Zhuhai, Huizhou
September 2003	Beijing, Shanghai
January 2004	Shantou, Chaoshan, Meizhou, Zhaoqing, Qingyuan, Yunfu
May 2004	Shanwei, Maoming, Zhanjiang, Yangjiang, Shaoguan, Jieyand, Heyuan
July 2004	Fuzhou, Xiamen, Quanzhou, Ninjing, Suzhou, Wuxi, Hangzhou, Ningbo, Taizhou
March 2005	Tianjin, Chongqing
November 2005	Chengdu, Jinan, Dalian, Shenyang
May 2006	Nanchang, Changsha, Nanning, Haikou, Guiyang, Kunming
July 2007	Shijiazhuang, Zhengzhou, Changchun, Hefei, Wuhan

and these infrastructures can be enjoyed by local residents. The costs include the pollution, increasing rent, overcrowding of tourist attractions and transportation services, etc., generated by the increase of tourists.

Macau: world gaming destination

Macau, Macao, or Ou Mun, is another Special Administration Region (SAR) in China. It is located on the east of Hong Kong and on the west of Pearl River Delta (PRD). It is considered as 'Monte Carlo of the Orient'. The population of Macau is less than one-tenth of Hong Kong (65 hundred thousand versus seven million) but it generated 78.1 billion dollars in 2018 and has the second highest GDP per capita in the world (International Monetary Fund, 2019). It is also one of the most densely populated areas in the world (Macao's Statistics and Census Services (DSEC), 2019). Macau became an official Portuguese colony in 1887 which returned to China in 1999. Since then, Macau has become a special administrative region according to the Joint Declaration on the Question of Macau and Macau Basic Law (DSEC, 2019). The Basic Law guarantees Macau to enjoy 'ne country, two systems' as in Hong Kong. It also allows Macau to be ruled with great autonomy. Ever since the return of Macau to China, the economy of Macau experienced enormous growth. Between 1999 and 2016, the GDP of Macau increased around seven times, from 51,872 million to 362,265 million (Sheng & Gu, 2018).

Unlike Hong Kong, which is a colony of the British for only 100 years, Macau has been under the influence of the Portuguese since 1550. The PortuguesePortuguese were the first to settle in Macau and with the permission of the Guangdong mandarins, the Portuguese established the city.

It became a major mid-point stop for trade between China, Japan, India, and Europe in a short period of time (Macao Government Tourism Office, 2019). After the Second Opium War (1860), trade between China and Western increased dramatically. However, Macau did not take advantage of this opportunity; it was outshined by Hong Kong during the same period. Macau turned itself to gambling (Porter, 1993). Hou Heng Company, a company leaded by Mr Fok, was the first company to receive a monopoly in the gaming industry. The first casino operated by Hou Heng is located in Avendia Almedia Riberiro and Tai Fung Bank. The company has improved the gaming sector via various innovation, such as the sumptuous renovation and refurbishment, complimentary opera shows, free food, cigarettes, snacks, and ferry tickets. Diploma Legistrativo no. 1496, a legislation designed to open the gaming monopoly for public bidding, was initiated by Governor Marques in 1961. Together with Tai Heng, the gaming company that was currently operating during that period, and a new company formed by Hon Ip, Terry Ip, Stanley Ho, and Henry Fok, there are two companies competing for the new monopoly. The new casino monopoly concessionaire was granted to Stanley Ho's Sociedade de Turismo e Diversões Macau (STDM) (Luo & Lam, 2018) in 1962. The first casino, Casino Estoril, was opened at the same time. The flagship Lisboa Hotel and Casino Lisboa was opened in 1970. This monopoly situation remains unchanged until the return of Macau to China. The Chief Executive, Mr Edmund Ho Hau Wah, on the day that Macau officials fell into the Chinese jurisdiction, announced a plan to invite experienced consultant agencies to research the perspective of the Macau gambling industry. In 2002, the Macau government terminated the monopoly and liberalized the gambling licences. Six licences were allocated to STDM, Wynn Macau, Las Vegas Sands, Galaxy Entertainment Group (a partnership of MGM Mirage and Pansy Ho, the daughter of Stanley Ho), and a partnership between Melco and Publishing and Broadcasting Limited (PBL). Many new hotels,resorts, and casinos were opened afterward. These foreign investors did not only bring western management skills, but also employment opportunities. Sands Macao, Wynn Macau, MGM Grand, Venetian Macau, and Galaxy Cotai Megaresort were opened in 2004, 2006, 2007, 2008, and 2011, respectively. Another mega resort, Lisboa Palace, was expected to open in late 2020. With only one-tenth of the size of Las Vegas (in terms of square kilometres) and 49 casinos (instead of 135 in Las Vegas), Macau does not only surpass Las Vegas, but it generates three times more in terms of gaming revenue (Guest, 2017). Figure 2.1 shows the number of tourist arrival and the number of tourists from Mainland China to Macau from 2008 to 2018. Figure 2.2 shows the percentage of tourists from Mainland China travelling to Macau

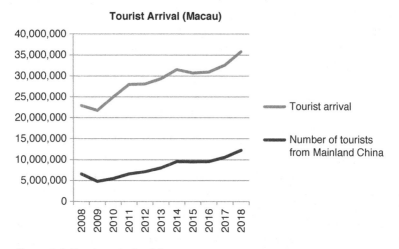

Figure 2.1 Tourist arrival to Macau.

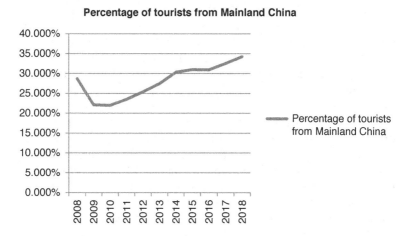

Figure 2.2 Percentage of tourists from Mainland China.

during the same period. As shown in Figure 2.2, the percentage of tourists from Mainland China increases continuously. This shows that Macau increases its reliance on tourists from Mainland China.

Macau also enjoys the benefit of the Individual Visit Scheme. When Hong Kong was suffering from the outbreak of SARS, the economy, particularly tourism in Macau took a hit. This is because many tourists would visit Macau and Hong Kong at the same time. To rescue or support the economy of Macau, the Chinese government allowed people from Mainland China to visit Macau on individual basis. Shortly after the implementation, the number of tourists' arrival to Macau increased from 5.7 million to 14.9 million in 2007 (Sheng & Gu, 2018). Similar to Hong Kong, after the implementation of IVS, Macau's economy becomes highly dependable on China. Both cities suffered from the challenges of limited tourist carrying capacity (Sheng & Gu, 2018). There were around 35 million visitors in 2018, which is 55 times more than Macau's population. However, unlike Hong Kong, Macau is dominating in gambling. The flux of visitors from Mainland China and the rest of the world, combined with international free flow of capital in Macau, provides ample opportunities for money laundering, corruption, etc. According to the Congressional-Executive Commission on China Annual Report (CECC, 2013), over 200 billion of 'ill-gotten funds' are laundered through Macau. The US Department of State identified Macau as one of the jurisdictions showing 'vulnerabilities for money laundering' (US Department of State, 2019). To address this, the Chinese government placed restrictions on visa applications to Macau in 2007 and 2008. The restrictions started from two visits per month to one visit every three months. In 2018, to avoid illegal use of Union Pay to circumvent foreign exchange control, the State Administration of Foreign Exchange in China imposed a limit of withdrawal to 10,000 RMB per day and 100,000 per year. Both measures affected Macau severely.

After the decrease in tourist arrival during the SARS epidemic in 2003 and financial crisis in 2008, the Macau and the Chinese government realized the importance of diversification, and that there was a risk of concentration in gambling. According to the twelfth Five-Year Plan, the Chinese government supported Macau's establishment as the 'World Tourism and Leisure Center'. Furthermore, the Guangdong–Macau Cooperation Framework Agreement stated that 'Macau is expected to transform from a largely casino gaming city to a more family and business travel destination' (Luo & Lam, 2018). The goal was to diversify the existing market and develop new markets, as well as new attractions. In 2008, Cirque du Soleil, a Canadian entertainment company and the largest theatrical producer in the world, launched ZAiA in Venetian Macau (Luo & Lam, 2019). Similar to many other successful shows in Las Vegas, such as KA in MGM Grand, O in Bellagio, and Mystere in Treasure Island, ZAiA is a residential show, which means the show performed regularly in the same location. However, due to various issues, including possible competition from another similar show, the *House of Dancing Water*, and low audience numbers, ZAiA was terminated in 2012. The *House of Dancing Water*, a show that combined dancing and circus performance, has been considered a recent success (Melco Crown, 2016). Despite the show bieng considered as a success in terms of audience and the associated benefits, such as attracting tourists to visit the resort, the corresponding expenditure associated with the visit compared to the revenue generated was minimal when compared with the gambling revenue. Therefore, these non-gambling activities are considered as a means (attracting visitors) to an end (gambling). In sum, the diversification process of Macau still has a long way to go. The success of Macau is not without trouble. Since gambling and tourism is the most important industry in Macau, the economy of Macau is highly influenced by globe's (especially China) economy and politics.

Guangdong tourism development

Guangdong Province or Canton Province is located in South China. It is the largest economic powerhouse in China (Zhang, Luo, Xiao, & Guillet, 2013). The GDP of Guangdong reached 9.73 trillion RMB in 2018 and around 87,000 GDP per capita (Guangdong Statistics and Information, 2019a). Guangdong has been generating the highest GDP among all provinces in China. It contains 21 cities and 1134 towns. With 113 million people living in Guangdong today, it is the seventh most dense area in China (National Bureau of Statistics of China, 2019). Since Guangdong contains five major airports and an efficient network of railways connecting with the rest of the country, Guangdong is one of the hottest tourist destinations in China. Guangdong can generally be classified into four regions, Pearl River Delta, Eastern Region, Western Region, and Mountainous Region. The most important region is Pearl River Delta (PRD), which contains Guangzhou, Shenzhen, Zhuhai, Foshan, Dongguan, Zhongshan, Jiangmen, Huizhou, and Zhaoqing.

In 1978, China adopted the Open Door Policy and Guangdong was the one of the few provinces to experience this. The Open Door Policy created Special Economic Zones (SEZ) to attract foreign investment. Among the first five SEZ created in 1978, two of which, Shenzhen and Zhuhai, were in Guangdong. These SEZ did not only bring foreign investment, when investors invested in these SEZ, they would also need to visit the site. This marks the beginning of inbound travel to Guangdong. Before the Open Door Policy, tourism in China primarily served the political purpose of promoting the achievement of Socialist China, expanding China's political influence, and promoting international understanding and friendship through receiving invited guest and tourists (Zhang, Chong, & Ap, 1999). After the Open Door Policy in 1978, foreigners were allowed to visit China. Since then, the nature of tourism gradually changed. Tourism became more economically orientated and the demand for tourism infrastructures increased accordingly. From 1981–1985, all levels, central, provincial, and local governments supported all organizations, collectives, and individuals to build tourism infrastructures and facilities with self-independence (Zhang, Pine & Lam, 2005). China's first theme park, the Shenzhen Splendid China Folk Culture Village, opened for business in Guangdong. The White Swan Hotel, the first five-star hotel in southern China, was built in 1990. Since the Open Door Policy, there has been a great influx of overseas tourists to Guangdong, and therefore a huge demand has been placed upon China's underdeveloped tourism industry. Guangdong is China's top international tourist destination. In 1980, there were only around 26,000 foreigners visiting Guangdong (Guangdong Statistic and Information, 2019a). In 2018over 27 million international tourists travelled to Guangdong, which represented 34 per cent of the total national inbound figure (China National Tourism Administration 2019). There were only around 600 hotels in 1990s, but in 2017, there were over 16,255 hotels (Statistical Bureau of Guangdong, 1991–2018), (see Table 2.3). In 2017, Guangdong welcomed over 36.5 million international tourists and around 408 million domestic tourists (see Figure 2.3).

According to the World Bank (2019), the GDP per capita increases from 1297 RMB in 1980 to over 65,000 RMB in 2018, as travelling became increasingly common for people in Guangdong. In addition, prior to the Individual Visit Scheme (IVS), Guangdong citizens were able to visit Hong Kong and Macau in 1984. The first batch of the IVS was given

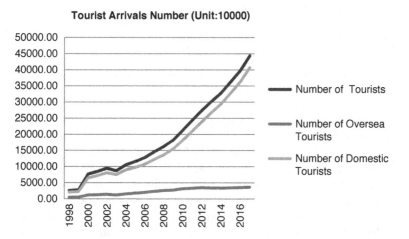

Figure 2.3 Number of tourists, number of oversea tourists and domestic tourists in Guangdong (1998–2017).

Source: Statistical Bureau of Guangdong (1999–2018).

Table 2.3 Number of star-rated hotels in Guangdong Province (1990–2017)

Year	Number of star-rated hotels					
	Total	Five Star	Four Star	Three Star	Two Star	One Star
1990	138	5	9	35	76	13
1991	210	5	10	52	120	23
1992	238	5	11	61	136	25
1993	264	8	12	78	143	23
1994	304	10	19	94	158	23
1995	338	10	20	121	168	19
1996	383	13	27	134	185	24
1997	406	15	31	143	191	26
1998	441	15	35	159	207	25
1999	455	15	40	171	205	24
2000	750	19	61	283	339	48
2001	931	28	86	351	415	51
2002	1008	30	93	382	448	55
2003	1095	33	112	426	468	56
2004	1071	39	124	452	418	38
2005	1128	41	140	496	412	39
2006	1164	47	158	555	372	32
2007	1171	58	168	575	344	26
2008	1165	69	177	592	307	20
2009	1181	79	193	626	270	13
2010	1220	94	205	661	246	14
2011	1156	102	198	651	197	8
2012	1092	107	187	630	160	8
2013	1083	115	187	629	145	7
2014	1012	119	184	589	115	5
2015	972	117	178	566	107	4
2016	861	110	162	498	87	4
2017	771	108	153	438	68	4

Sources: Statistical Bureau of Guangdong, 1991–2018.

to many cities in Guangdong. Guangdong's tourism industry grew quickly afterwards. According to the Statistical Bureau of Guangdong (2012), there were 1349 travel agents in 2011. Tourism became one of the pillar industries in 2009 and was incorporated into the twelfth Five Year Plan (2011–2015). With the opening of High-Speed-Rail become accessible in many cities, the opening of Hong Kong-Zhuhai-Macau Bridge, a 55 km bridge connecting the three cities, in 2018, and the Shenzhen-Zhongshan Bridge expected to be completed by 2024, people in all cities in China will be able to travel around more conveniently.

China's tourism has developed rapidly since its initiation of the reform and the Open Door Policy. However, as is also the case with broader economic development in China, both domestic and international tourist activities are heavily concentrated on the coastal gateways. Demurger (2000) believed that the openness and reform policies were not applied to all provinces at the same rate. At first, the policy was applied only to selected coastal provinces, such as Guangdong and Fujian. These provinces were intended to become the engines for the growth progress in China. Foreign investment and export expansion increased rapidly in the coastal regions. Inland regions were left behind. Hong Kong has been active in acting as an intermediary between foreign investors and the PRD, as well as the rest of Mainland China (Constitutional and Mainland Affairs Bureau, 2006). The PRD became one of the most important manufacturing centre in the world and one of the country's fastest growing regions. However, due to the physical distance between Hong Kong and some of the PRD regions, such as Zhuhai, Zhongshan, Jiangmen, Foshan, and Zhaoqing, CMAB (2006) showed that these cities suffered from a relatively weaker infrastructure than the rest of cities in the PRD region. Qian, Wang, and Wu (2012) reported that there was regional disparity in tourism development between the Southeast coast and the Northwest inland cities. Although the overall tourism development improved significantly during the last few decades, there was still a significant difference between the coastal and inland areas. One purpose of the development of Greater Bay Area, is to further integrate all cities in the PRD region with Hong Kong and Macau. The Hong Kong-Macau-Zhuhai Bridge, Shenzhen-Zhongshan Bridge, and the High-Speed Railway are ways to connect the cities more efficiently.

Summary

This chapter briefly summarized the historical development of Hong Kong, Macau, and Guangdong discussing policies, economics, and tourism. Hong Kong has been a traditional international hub connecting the PRD and the rest of the world. Macau has been a traditional gaming city with the urge to diversify its economy. Guangdong has been developed into a manufacturing centre and a popular tourist destination with the hope to spread the prosperity to other regions. The Individual Visit Scheme along with the newly built Hong Kong-Macau-Zhuhai Bridge and many other infrastructures will further integrate the nine cities in the PRD regions, Hong Kong, and Macau into the Greater Bay Area.

References

CECC (2013). 2013 Annual Report. [Online]. Retrieved 1 February 2020, from www.cecc.gov/publications/annual-reports/2013-annual-report

Census and Statistics Department (2018). *Hong Kong Annual Disgest of Statistics (2018 Edition).* Retrieved 30 June 2019 from www.censtatd.gov.hk/fd.jsp? file=B10100032018AN18B0100.pdf&product_id=B1010003&lang=1China National Tourism Administration (2019). The Yearbook of China Tourism Statistics. China Travel and Tourism Press, Peking.

Choi, S. W. (2007). From fishing port to 'City of Life': Hong Kong history according to the Hong Kong Tourism Board. *Cultural Studies@ Lingnan, 3*(1), 1–23.

Commerce and Economic Development Bureau. (2019). *Individual Visit Scheme.* Retrieved 30 June 2019 from www.tourism.gov.hk/english/visitors/visitors_ind. html

Constitutional and Mainland Affairs Bureau (CMAB) (2006). *The Development of Western Pearl River Delta Region and its Prospects for Collaboration with Hong Kong.* Retrieved 12 July 2019 from www.cmab.gov.hk/doc/study_report_ on_the_development_of_western_prd_eng.pdf

Demurger, S. (2000). *Economic opening and growth in China. OECD development centre studies.* Paris: OECD.

Education Bureau. (2019). *Individual Visit Scheme in Hong Kong.* Retrieved 30 June 2019 from www.edb.gov.hk/attachment/en/curriculum-development/kla/ pshe/references-and-resources/economics/IVS_eng.pdf

GovHK (2019). *Hong Kong.* Retrieved 19 June 2019 www.gov.hk/en/about/ abouthk/factsheets/docs/population.pdf

Guangdong Statistics and Information (2019a). *Guangdong Economic and Social Development Statistics Report in 2018.* Retrieved 11 July 2019 from www. gdstats.gov.cn/tjzl/tjgb/201902/t20190227_423113.html

Guangdong Statistics and Information (2019b). *Guangdong Economic and Social Development Statistics Report in 2018.* Retrieved 11 July 2019 from www. gdstats.gov.cn/tjzl/tjgb/201712/t20171209_377708.html

Guest, P. (2017). *More Over Vegas, Macau is Now the Gambling Capital of the World.* Retrieved 21 December 2019, from www.valuewalk.com/2017/10/ gambling-revenue/

Hong Kong Economy (2005). *Hong Kong's tourism industry.* Retrieved 19 June 2019 from www.hkeconomy.gov.hk/en/pdf/box-05q1-3-1.pdf

HK Government News (2011). *Four traditional activities from Hong Kong successfully inscribed to the national list of intangible cultural heritage.* Retrieved 20 June 2019 from www.info.gov.hk/gia/general/201106/03/P201106030233.htm

Hong Kong Tourism Board (HKTB) (2003–2019). *Annual Report.* Retrieved 19 June 2019 from www.discoverhongkong.com/eng/about-hktb/images/2003-2004-05.pdf

Hong Kong Tourism Board (HKTB) (2019a). *About Hong Kong Tourism Board.* Retrieved 19 June 2019 from www.discoverhongkong.com/eng/about-hktb/ index.jsp

Hong Kong Trade Development Council (HKTDC) (2019), *Hong Kong Advantage.* Retrieved 20 June 2019 from https://hkmb.hktdc.com/en/venture-hong-kong/ hong-kong-advantage

International Monetary Fund (IMF) (2019). *Macau.* Retrieved 9 July 2019 from www.imf.org/external/pubs/ft/weo/2018/02/weodata/weorept.aspx?pr.

x=39&pr.y=11&sy=2018&ey=2018&scsm=1&ssd=1&sort=country&ds=.&br=
1&c=546&s=NGDP%2CNGDPD%2CPPPGDP%2CNGDPPC%2CNGDPDPC
%2CPPPPC&grp=0&a=

Luo, J. M. (Ed.). (2016). *Urbanization and tourism development in China.* Nova Science Publishers, Incorporated.

Luo, J. M., & Lam, C. F. (Eds). (2016). *Corporate Social Responsibility and Responsible Gambling in Gaming Destinations.* Nova Science Publishers, Incorporated.

Luo, J. M., & Lam C. F. (2018). *Entertainment Tourism.* New York: Routledge.

Luo, J. M., & Lam, C. F. (2019). The Examination of Entertainment Product Performance in Macau. ICHRIE Research Report, 1–3.

Macao Government Tourism Office. (2019). *About Macao.* Retrieved 9 July 2019 from http://en.macaotourism.gov.mo/plan/aboutmacao_detail.php?id=1

Macao's Statistics and Census Services (DSEC) (2019). *Macao in figures.* Retrieved 9 July 2019 from www.dsec.gov.mo/Statistic.aspx?NodeGuid=ba1a 4eab-213a-48a3-8fbb-962d15dc6f87

Melco Crown. (2016). About us. Retrieved 1 July, 2019, from www.melco-crown. com/eng/bg.php

National Bureau of Statistics of China. (2019). *National Data.* Retrieved 11 July 2019 from http://data.stats.gov.cn/english/easyquery.htm?cn=E0103

Porter, J. (1993). The transformation of Macau. *Pacific Affairs,* 7–20.

Qian, L., Wang, Y., & Wu, W. (2012). The differences and changes of Provincial Tourism Development in China. Tourism Tribune, 27(1), 31–38.

Sheng, M., & Gu, C. (2018). Economic growth and development in Macau (1999–2016): The role of the booming gaming industry. *Cities, 75,* 72–80.

Statistical Bureau of Guangdong (1991–2018). *Guangdong Statistical Yearbook.* China Statistics Press, Beijing.

UNWTO (2018). *UNWTO Tourism Highlights (2018 Edition).* Retrieved 19 June 2019 from www.e-unwto.org/doi/pdf/10.18111/9789284419876

US Department of State (2019). *2019 International Narcotics Control Strategy Report.* Retrieved 9 July 2019 from www.state.gov/2019-international-narcotics-control-strategy-report/

Yen. Z. (September, 2017). *The Global Financial Centres Index 22.* Retrieved 19 June 2019 from www.longfinance.net/media/documents/gfci_22.pdf

Yen. Z. (March 2019). *The Global Financial Centres Index 25.* Retrieved 19 June 2019 from www.longfinance.net/media/documents/GFCI_25_Report.pdf

Zhang, H. Q., Chong, K., & Ap, J. (1999). An analysis of tourism policy development in modern China. *Tourism Management, 20*(4), 471–485.

Zhang, H. Q., Luo, J. M., Xiao, Q., & Guillet, B. D. (2013). The impact of urbanization on hotel development: Evidence from Guangdong Province in China. *International Journal of Hospitality Management,* 34, 92–98.

Zhang, H. Q. Ray Pine, & Terry Lam. (2005). *Tourism and Hotel Development in China: from political to economic success.* New York: Psychology Press.

3 City integration in the Greater Bay Area

Defining city integration

City integration means a city cooperating with nearby cities to form common institutions and laws. This cooperation can be in forms of common agreement or mutual recognition from economic and political environments. The objective of the agreement or recognition usually focuses on commercial interests, as well as socio-political and security objectives through political economy initiatives. City integration typically takes the form of reducing trade barriers, increasing labour, capitals, and product mobility, and adopting cohesive stances on policy issues, such as environment, climate change, and migration. Many 'satellite' cities in Europe eventually converged via city integration to form a large urban centre for a particular purpose, such as universities, incubators, industries, transportation hubs, and military bases. Well-known examples include Greater London, Greater Paris, Helsinki Espoo (Finland), and Sandnes–Stavanger (Norway).

The origin of city integration can be traced back to the term 'city-region' used by Geddes (1915). 'City-region' was used to describe how nearby cities become interconnected spatially and administratively through city networks, which are channels for cities to exchange people, goods and services, capital, idea and knowledge. Ultimately, the integrated cities become 'more than the sum of its parts' (Meijers, 2005: 765). Many researchers focused on the features that arose during city integration via city networks. Camagni and Capello (2004) found that city networks depend on physical integration, such as transportation hub, and functional integration, such as the exchange of information and capital. Other researchers further divided information integration to innovation and knowledge integration and claimed that both are also important to city integrations (Cooke, 2001; Krätke & Brandt, 2009).

State rescaling is a crucial perspective for understanding urban and regional restructuring (Brenner, 2009; Park, 2013). The rescaling of the state and privileging of city-regions are part and parcel of neoliberal agendas to position major cities and strategic city-regions within global circuits of capital accumulation (Brenner, 2004). State rescaling is valuable to city planners for configuring the corresponding spatial and scalar organization in a city to control urban and regional development under continuously modifying political and economic environments (Harrison, 2014). Transformation does not require elimination of entire political geographies of the region but is forged by combining regional policies and projects with specific historical and spatial states in a complex manner (Brenner, 2004: 107). Harrison (2012) showed that the initiation of city-regional governance does not mean city-regional scale should be prioritized over others. Rather, it should be part of a multiplication of governance scaling. Rescaling is difficult. The construction of cities does not simply involve enlargement of state, but a political influence from bottom to top (Cox, 2009; Klink, 2013).

Regional city integration in the Greater Bay Area

The Pearl River Delta metropolitan region

The Pearl River Delta (PRD) is a region located in Guangdong Province where the Pearl River flows into the South China Sea. Since China's economic reforms commenced in 1979, the PRD in southern China has become one of the most dynamic regions for economic development, establishing itself as one of the most affluent areas in China and one of the most densely populated urban areas in the world. The PRD region is composed of cities in southern China, with a total of over 50,000 km^2 in area and over 60 million people. The PRD economic zone is one of China's leading economic regions and a major manufacturing centre. It is located at the Pearl River estuary where the river enters the South China Sea. The zone is formed by nine cities, namely, Guangzhou (the provincial capital), Shenzhen, Foshan, Zhuhai, Jiangmen, Zhongshan, Dongguan, Huizhou, and Zhaoqing. The nine cities of the PRD had a combined population of 61.50 million at the end of 2018, comprising 55.07 per cent of the Guangdong provincial population (Statistical Bureau of Guangdong, 2018) (see Table 3.1).

The PRD was the earliest beneficiary of the reform and opening up policy proposed by the late Chinese leader Mr Deng Xiaoping in the late 1970s. The PRD has been leading the country in most economic indices in the past three decades, including those related to tourism being (Huang, Li, Zheng, & Li, 2006). A series of efforts towards cooperation within the region have been undertaken during the past 40 years, culminating in the

Table 3.1 Profile of Greater Bay Area

Item	Pearl River Delta	East Wing	West Wing	Mountainous areas
Land area (sq.km.)	54,770	15,476	32,646	76,751
Permanent population at the year-end (10,000 persons)	6,150.54	1,732.26	1,605.20	1,681.00
Urban population (10,000 persons)	5,245.70	1,040.57	698.66	816.54
Employed persons at the year-end (10,000 persons)	3,981.41	759.62	757.79	841.96
Gross domestic product (100 million yuan)	75,710.14	6,202.54	7,022.40	5,539.75
Primary industry	1,181.53	455.36	1,172.86	800.36
Secondary industry	31,542.82	3,115.66	2,674.70	1,973.38
Tertiary industry	42,985.80	2,631.53	3,174.84	2,766.01
Per capita GDP (yuan)	124,564	35,844	43,922	33,039

Sources: Statistical Bureau of Guangdong, 2018.

institutional arrangement of the 'Pan Pearl River Delta Cooperation Plan' in 2004, which was officially recognized and prioritized by the Chinese central government (Liang & Zhang, 2006). Sophisticated degrees of cooperation have been achieved within the delta in several areas of manufacturing, including textiles and electronics, food safety, disease control, and public security management. However, dire and even 'internecine', competition has also been spotted particularly, in road and bridge construction, environmental protection, and service industries, including logistics and finance. Problems related to competition have also arisen in rivalling government preferential policies for attracting foreign investment in terms of land, tax, and utility incentives and, regrettably, environmental and labour regulations (Zhang, Yan, & Lo, 2009).

Economic integration

The factories of the PRD have been termed as the 'World's Factories' because of the large amount of foreign investment in the region. The PRD started producing labour-intensive consumer goods such as food and beverages, toys and clothes in the early 1980s. After 1985, industrial relocation, mainly from Hong Kong, accelerated the growth of light industry in PRD until early 1990s. Following, heavy industry, featuring high-tech electronic equipment and machinery, chemical products and autos played a leading role in industrial output and export. As a manufacturing base of the world, the region plays a leading role in several industries. Some categories of the toy industry in the PRD have a world production share

Table 3.2 Main economic indicators of the Pearl River Delta Economic Zone

Year	Permanent population at the year-end (10,000 persons)	Urban population	Total population with residence registration at the year-end (10,000 persons)	Employed persons at the year-end (10,000 persons)	Employed persons in urban areas
1990	2369.93	1696.63	2371.57		
1995	3292.03		2372.76		
2000	4289.78	2981.23	2563.60	1902.93	495.46
2001	4376.10		2595.24	1947.10	480.97
2002	4414.68		2624.93	2034.09	498.78
2003	4463.55		2660.46	2250.43	523.34
2004	4516.50		2714.08	2492.27	570.64
2005	4547.14	3516.06	2763.32	2822.60	636.10
2006	4735.47	3771.33	2821.27	2963.93	675.38
2007	4930.68	3919.89	2872.47	3107.38	718.88
2008	5138.48	4119.52	2920.82	3232.88	724.38
2009	5361.72	4375.17	2967.02	3412.10	767.05
2010	5616.39	4645.88	3024.57	3572.01	823.67
2011	5646.51	4687.17	3073.87	3630.21	927.40
2012	5689.64	4770.19	3105.01	3638.83	969.59
2013	5715.19	4802.55	3156.02	3784.09	1552.80
2014	5763.38	4848.41	3207.94	3845.25	1555.45
2015	5874.27	4969.10	3265.69	3871.26	1532.73
2016	5998.49	5089.64	3350.52	3926.93	1547.13
2017	6150.54	5245.70	3475.10	3981.41	1560.00
2018	6300.99	5413.11	3628.04	4146.60	1603.20

Sources: Statistical Bureau of Guangdong, 2018.

exceeding 60 per cent. Other leading products include footwear, lighting fixtures, and furniture.

Despite the mature light industry, the PRD is shifting its emphasis to heavy industry. In terms of gross output value, Guangdong's ratio of light industry to heavy industry (above designated size) has turned from 1.39:1 in 1995 to 0.60:1 in 2016. Plans are in place to encourage relocation of labour-intensive industries in the PRD to peripheral areas and develop telecom, equipment manufacture, auto and petrochemical industries in PRD. Heavy industries are emerging in the PRD, especially in Guangzhou and Huizhou. Guangzhou is becoming one of the three auto manufacturing bases in China. The number of sedan cars produced in Guangdong reached 2.6 million in 2016, accounting for 21.7 per cent of the national total. The plant set up by *Honda* in 1998 initiated the auto and part cluster in Guangzhou. *Nissan* and *Toyota* and business cars specialist *Hyundai* joined later. Many world-famous auto part manufacturers are locating in nearby areas, such as Japan's biggest car part maker, Denso. Other PRD cities surrounding Guangzhou are developing the auto part industry by establishing development zones, for example, in Foshan, Zhongshan, Shenzhen, and Huizhou Daya Bay. Over the past three decades, the composition of economy has experienced a typical change with the increased contribution of tertiary industries to the economy. Increased affluence on the part of residents has fuelled demand for services such as education, recreation, travelling, and telecom services. In recent years, business services have also been burgeoning in the PRD, together with the rapid growth of secondary industries. The pace of foreign investment in services has actually sped up, concomitant to China's further liberalization.

As part of its push for a balanced economic growth across the country, the Chinese government has been actively promoting the development of inland provinces. In the past three decades, the government has allowed the coastal provinces to develop and get rich first. This course of action has resulted in a widening prosperity gap between first-tier cities like Shanghai, Beijing, Shenzhen, and Guangzhou, and the rest of the country. The wave of immigrant workers leaving their families behind in inland provinces to pursue better job opportunities in big cities and university graduates staying in cities to earn better incomes have further led to a concentration of wealth. To rebalance growth, the government has invested heavily in infrastructure and offered business migration incentives to attract cost-conscious PRD businesses to relocate to inland provinces whilst encouraging higher-end producers looking for qualified yet expensive talent to stay in the PRD.

Restructuring the PRD economy from 'made in Guangdong' to 'created in Guangdong' is at the heart of the government plans (Yeung, 2010).

They envision accomplishing this in two ways. First, the government plans to upgrade traditional industries. Specifically, it plans to modernize strategically important capital-intensive industries, including manufacturing equipment, autos, steel, petrochemicals, shipbuilding, and power generation equipment. The focus is on making industry structure leaner and more efficient, improving the variety and quality of products and enhancing industry innovation. In addition, the government plans to upgrade other traditional manufacturing industries, including household electronics, textiles and garments, food and beverages, construction materials, paper and Chinese medicine, so that they can compete with global brands. Second, the PRD will be the testing ground for emerging high-tech as well as service industries. These include information and communication technologies (ICTs), biotechnology, new materials, environmental technologies and marine technology. The Guangdong government also plans to cultivate breakthrough innovations, cooperating with industry players in areas ranging from broadband technologies, modern Chinese medicine and bioinformatics, electric vehicles, LED technologies, and material science to various green technologies (Altrock & Schoon, 2013). In terms of services, the PRD's planned focus will be financial services, conventions and exhibitions, logistics, IT and high-tech services, outsourcing, creative industries, headquarter services and tourism (Altrock & Schoon, 2013). Movement towards industrial upgrading and the development of new industries has already begun: last year, the Guangdong government launched over 500 projects with a total investment of RMB 1.2 trillion focused on upgrading the region's innovation capacity. Approximately 100 projects focused on strategic emerging industries, advanced manufacturing, modern service industries, upgrading of traditional industries and modern agriculture. More than 90 per cent of the projects have already begun with the construction. Additionally, new industrial clusters are planned for Shenzhen, Qianhai, Zhuhai, Hengqin, Guangzhou, Nansha, and Hetao. This year, Guangdong province has also signed new investment agreements worth over RMB 2 trillion with 70 state-owned enterprises on more than 200 projects to modernize traditional industries, more than doubling the previous amount invested in this area (Council, 2011).

The Guangdong Free Trade Zone (FTZ) was officially opened in April 2015 and is located in the Nansha District of Guangzhou. The FTZ is approximately 116 km^2 and extends into Qianhai–Shekou and Hengqin areas (Statistical Bureau of Guangdong, 2018). The FTZ operates similarly to the other Chinese FTZ, offering a more open regulatory environment to encourage more foreign investment in the area. The establishment of the FTZ allows for the formation of foreign-owned shipping enterprises in the PRD, and encourages enterprises and financial institutions to loan money overseas. It also encourages the cooperation of businesses in Hong Kong and Macau to invest in the PRD area. Looking forward, these developments will certainly play a key role in the continued growth of the PRD economy.

Social integration

Speeding up the introduction of new concepts to the social management system for the PRD region, Guangdong Province gradually extends the pilot scheme on social management system reform and encourages the PRD cities to consider making changes to their social management and public services systems to best suit their local situation. Mainly, to consider restructuring government functions, improving relevant legislations and regulations, establishing government service procurement systems, setting up and engaging non-governmental or resident organizations in social management; to promote the development of non-governmental organizations by improving their registration and management system; to help establish social worker teams; to create new mechanisms for urban and rural community management to allow self-management and promote self-service; to reform the household management systems by allowing more opportunities for the migrant population to participate in social and local affairs management and to establish a migrant registration system unique to the PRD with a view to progressively stabilizing regional population growth and enhancing the population structure (see Figure 3.1).

Efforts in the education sector further supplement this push for change. The Guangdong government aims to increase school enrolment and enhance the calibre of higher education by inviting international players to Guangdong. Thus far, the University of Birmingham has announced plans to launch a Guangzhou centre, whereas Guangzhou, Zhuhai, and Shenzhen plan to establish cooperative programs with three to five well-known foreign universities by 2020 (Council, 2011).

Environmental integration

The PRD has built a complete network for water, land, and air transportation. Cities in the PRD are interconnected by highways and railways. The PRD is improving its land network to strengthen linkages among cities. According to the Outline of the Plan for the Reform and Development of the PRD promulgated in 2009, the PRD will speed up its inter-city rail transportation network and strengthen the transportation linkage between the east and west bank of the Pearl River. Ports in the PRD play a critical role for transporting manufactured goods abroad. With its geographical

Figure 3.1 Living communities in Dongguan City.

advantage, the PRD has built excellent port facilities, including coastal ports and ports of inland rivers. Major ports in the PRD include Guangzhou Port, Yantian Port, Shekou Port, and Chiwan Port of Shenzhen. In 2018, the ports of Shenzhen were the world's third busiest container seaport after Shanghai and Singapore (Statistical Bureau of Guangdong, 2018).

Regarding land transportation, the PRD has over 63,630 km of highways. In 2018, the PRD had a total of 11.37 million private vehicles, accounting for about 76 per cent of Guangdong's total. As far as connection to Hong Kong is concerned, it takes just two hours from Guangzhou to Hong Kong by train. The Hong Kong-Shenzhen Western Corridor had been put into use as the fourth vehicular land crossing between Shenzhen and Hong Kong. Besides, the new 'Y-shaped' bridge connecting Hong Kong, Macau, and Zhuhai is expected to boost the economy in the west PRD by improving its accessibility to Hong Kong. Since the operation of Shenzhen Metro in December 2004, Hong Kong and other cities in the PRD area are now interconnected by subway and rails. By 2018, the express rail link will be established between Guangzhou, Shenzhen, and

Hong Kong, and the travel time from Hong Kong to Guangzhou will be significantly reduced to 48 minutes. There are four airports in the PRD. The Baiyun Airport in Guangzhou is one of the three air hubs of China. In 2018, the passenger traffic of the Baiyun airport surpassed 59.7 million and volume of freight handled over 2.15 million tonnes. The Shenzhen International Airport has also grown considerably in the past decade with a passenger traffic over 41.9 million, and the volume of freight handled up to 1.13 million tons. The future development of roads and transportation infrastructure in Shenzhen will provide opportunities for easier travel and flow of goods. The Shenzhen-Zhongshan Bridge is currently planned to connect the two largest cities in the PRD. This bridge will cut travel times between the two cities to 30 minutes (Statistical Bureau of Guangdong, 2018).

To ensure better use of land supply for promoting changes in the pattern of economic development, the following should be done: actively promote 'double transfers' within Guangdong, i.e. relocating population and industries between the PRD region and the eastern, western, and northern parts of Guangdong Province, as well as between the core and peripheral areas of the PRD region; promote better planning and distribution of industries and more balanced development of the region; for places where industries are to be relocated to, put more emphasis on energy conservation, emissions reduction, as well as environmental protection so as to minimize the environmental impacts brought about by the relocation of industries; for service-oriented cities, encourage their development as public transportation hubs and become multi-functional centres with commercial facilities, offices, hotels, apartments, leisure facilities, and so on; for the PRD region, formulate criteria for industrial land use and development taking account of the level of technological innovation, investment, production and output, energy usage and emissions, and infrastructure required for supporting circular economy and promote upgrading of trades and industries, facilitate more integrated development for industrial parks and urban cities, and accelerate the development of service-oriented economies and creative industries.

Hong Kong and Shenzhen

The economic integration of Hong Kong Special Administrative Region (SAR) with the mainland has primarily taken place in the PRD. Hong Kong SAR's role as a producer's services and finance hub will depend on frictionless movements of goods, services, people, and know-how, requiring policy coordination to further promote trade and investment and developing a common human skill base with the PRD. Regional cooperation will also be needed to minimize the costs of rising levels of cross-border pollution. By contrast, the city of Shenzhen has a remarkable recent history. In the 1970s when Shenzhen had barely 30,000 residents, it was a market and fishing town located on the Kowloon–Canton Railway. This changed in 1979 when the Chinese Government assigned its city status, and then in 1980 when it was designated as the first special economic zone (SEZ). Over the past 40 years, Shenzhen's population increased over 300 times giving it the name 'The Instant City', and this is primarily because it was designated as a SEZ. A SEZ is designed to be free-market oriented by offering tax incentives for foreign investment and more freedoms for international trade.

Economic integration

Although many cities in the Greater Bay Area (GBA) are manufacture-based, Hong Kong follows a slightly different path. Since Hong Kong was a colony of the United Kingdom after its return to China in 1997, Hong Kong enjoys 'one country, two systems'. This special arrangement allows Hong Kong to follow British Common Law instead of the Constitution in China. This special arrangement, combined with the freest economy in the world, allowed Hong Kong to continue to be the gateway to China during the twentieth century. During this period, Hong Kong focused on finance, logistics, trading, investment, and management services, many manufacturing industries originally based in Hong Kong moved to Shenzhen or other areas in the GBA to take advantage of the geographic convenience and low labour cost. Hong Kong is now a knowledge-based service economy focused on exporting goods manufactured in the GBA via its international trading networks and providing professional services to those companies that want international business.

The twelfth Five-Year Plan has an entire chapter devoted to Hong Kong, compared to the single paragraph in the eleventh Five-Year Plan and one sentence in the tenth Five-Year Plan. The Chinese government promises to support Hong Kong's development as an offshore RMB centre, in addition to continuing to build on its strengths in finance, trade, logistics, shipping, tourism, and professional services particularly to help speed up the economic restructuring of mainland PRD cities such as Shenzhen, Guangzhou, and Dongguan. Hong Kong also plans to develop six new pillar industries, with significant collaboration with other Guangdong cities. The Chinese government has reiterated its vision for Hong Kong to build on its strength as an international financial centre. Hong Kong already has the largest RMB liquidity pool outside mainland China.

The GDP of Hong Kong in 2018 reached 2845.3 billion (HKD) or 2400 billion (RMB), whereas the GDP of Shenzhen reached 2422.2 billion

(RMB), which is higher than Hong Kong's GDP by roughly 22 billion (RMB). This was the first time Shenzhen exceeded Hong Kong and became the city with the highest GDP within the GBA. However, even when Shenzhen exceeds Hong Kong, Hong Kong continues to enjoy many advantages, such as the degree of openness, jurisdiction, and business environment. Shenzhen still has much to learn from Hong Kong (see Figure 3.2). Foreign enterprises, most of which from Hong Kong, accounted for about half of Guangdong's total exports in 2018. Shenzhen, Dongguan, and Guangzhou, thanks to their proximity to Hong Kong, are the three cities in the PRD that attracted the most foreign direct investment (FDI). Liao, Dai and Li (2019)reported that the education, technology, and culture of Hong Kong, as well as its ability to allocate resources internationally well exceed the ability of Shenzhen. During the development of the GBA, the degree of integration between Hong Kong and Shenzhen decide the position and level of the GBA among other major cities in the world.

Qianhai (Shenzhen–Hong Kong Modern Service Industry Cooperation Zone) is a commercial development in Shenzhen, Guangdong that is also

Figure 3.2 Overview of Hong Kong.

known as Qianhai New District. Qianhai is situated in the PRD. With the completion of railways and roads by 2020, Qianhai will be within a one-hour commuting radius of the PRD and within a 30-minute commuting radius of Hong Kong. The main arteries of traffic in the region, including the Shenzhen–Zhongshan corridor, Shenzhen Western Port, Shenzhen North Station, and Guangzhou–Shenzhen Yanjiang Highway, which all pass through Qianhai. According to plans made by the Qianhai administration, it will be the pilot district for cooperation between mainland China and Hong Kong, and innovation in the service industry. An example of Qianhai's future work environment, the Qianhai Enterprise Dream Park is modelled after the Silicon Valley, with 58 office buildings and a multipurpose building that can be used as a conference and exhibition hall and an exchange platform. Companies planning to move in, or have already moved in, include the Hong Kong and Shanghai Banking Corporation, Hang Seng Bank, Industrial and Commercial Bank of China and China Mobile. Although some companies have moved in, construction is ongoing. The Hong Kong government is planning to develop a bridgehead economy on Lantau Island to relieve some of the city's burden in the downtown areas, whilst paving the way for a third-generation central business district should Kowloon East also reach its capacity in the future. The Hong Kong–Zhuhai–Macau bridge will also shorten the physical connections. The greater delta is set to become a key tourism node for Asia, and business travellers will find it easier to commute between Hong Kong and Qianhai. A potential 16–18 million square metres of office space will be built and occupied by enterprises in Qianhai, and all will be only 30 minutes away from Hong Kong (Qianhai Media Center, 2019).

Social integration

The national Five-Year Plan also supports the development of a Shenzhen–Hong Kong Innovation Circle to expand collaboration in R&D and production. Thus far, Shenzhen-based BYD, which specializes in electric vehicles (EVs) and rechargeable batteries, has set up a new R&D facility in the Hong Kong Science Park to develop EVs for public transport. Universities in the United Kingdom and Germany have set up research and engineering laboratories partnering with research institutes in Hong Kong and Shenzhen. For instance, Southampton University has set up a web science laboratory with Tsinghua University's graduate school in Shenzhen (Council, 2011). Beijing Genomics Institute (BGI) has collaborated with the University of Hong Kong on the genomic sequencing of a scarlet fever pathogen, as well as with University Medical Center Hamburg-Eppendorf on the genomic sequencing of a rare *E. coli* strain originating in

Germany that has infected thousands of people since May 2011 (Council, 2011).

Shenzhen also has two 24/7 roads that cross the border into Hong Kong at Huanggang and Lok Ma Chau. These roads create an interesting dynamic with Hong Kong being an SAR and at these two locations people can pass through by car, bus, or a pedestrian walkway. To improve the quality of life for people living across boundaries, the following should be done: continuously improve the cross-boundary coordination and cooperation mechanism in the provision of social services so as allow the three sides to capitalize on their resources and strengths and complement each other's role; encourage social service providers to operate across boundaries and establish suitable mechanisms to safeguard the welfare of people living across boundaries, and enhance their convenience of living.

Adjusting land supply and land-use planning to improve the quality of life: Guangdong Province should carry out in-depth investigation on housing needs to progressively develop mechanisms for providing diversified housing for meeting the different needs of the community, and ensuring adequate land supply; to progressively establish a land use protection system; to continue to develop greenways in the PRD region, including expansion and improvement of the regional greenway networks, progressively developing urban and communal greenway systems, connecting cities and communities with greenway networks, and establishing extensive ecological corridors between urban and rural areas; to uphold the principle of preserving natural landscapes and conserving ecology during establishment of greenways so as to maintain and strengthen the foundation of the natural ecology; for Hong Kong, to continue to implement and strengthen existing measures on nature conservation in Hong Kong, which includes the designation of country parks, special areas, marine parks, coastal protection areas and conservation areas, as well as carrying out conservation planning for important habitats and species.

Environment integration

Shenzhen Railway Station is located along the border of Hong Kong and is the primary hub for inter-city trains in the Guangdong Province. Futian Railway Station is the most recently opened main railway station in Shenzhen and was completed in 2015. It is the largest underground station in Asia and the second largest in the world. Futian Railway Station is located in the centre of the Futian District and has three different levels. Level 1 holds the concourses for the metro, high speed and inter-city trains along with an immigration check point. Level 2 is for all Shenzhen metro trains and Level 3 is for the high-speed trains. Shenzhen North Railway Station is located at Longhua and serves as an interchange between the Guangzhou–Shenzhen–Hong Kong Express Rail Link and the Hangzhou–Fuzhou–Shenzhen High–Speed Railway. This station handles long distance trains to cities all over China including key routes to Guangzhou, Changsha, and Beijing. Shenzhen West Station was originally built in 1993, but was renovated and expanded in 2003. Due to Shenzhen largely being a migrant city, Shenzhen West Station's passenger demand has grown and now it handles a 45 per cent capacity of all passengers travelling to and from Shenzhen by rail. The Pingshan Railway Station is located in the Pingshan New District and the high-speed railway (HSR) station on the Xiamen–Shenzhen Railway (Statistical Bureau of Guangdong, 2018).

Bao'an International Airport situated 23 km outside of the city centre was opened in 1991, and it serves Shenzhen. Being the fourth busiest airport in China, demand from passengers and airlines for routes is considerable. Bao'an International Airport is also a hub for Shenzhen Airlines, Hainan Airlines, SF Airlines, Donghai Airlines, and UPS Airlines. As one of the three largest airports in the PRD, Bao'an International Airport also has a ferry service that connects it to Hong Kong International Airport allowing travellers to avoid going in and out of immigration and customs when transiting for a connecting flight. Shenzhen Bao'an International Airport has connections to most major cities in China but a number of international destinations, particularly in Asia (including Tokyo, Seoul, and Pyongyang).

The Shenzhen Port is located in the PRD and is divided by the Kowloon Peninsula. As a key SEZ, the Shenzhen Port houses a large market for imports and exports. The eastern port is situated along the Dapeng Bay, and the western port is close to Lingdinyang, approximately 40 km from Hong Kong and 110 km from Guangzhou. The most accessible route to Shenzhen is through the Shekou Passenger Terminal, which connects the city to the other key destinations in the PRD. Destinations include Hong Kong (25 nautical miles), Hong Kong International Airport (11 nautical miles), Macau–Yeutong Terminal (32 nautical miles), Macau–New HK Macau Ferry Terminal (25 nautical miles), and Zhuhai (25 nautical miles).

Hong Kong and Shenzhen plan to coordinate regional ecological protection work in this area, and raise the protection grading; increasing and enhancing protection of vegetation cover in this area by making reference to the management model of the nature conservation area under the terrestrial vegetation ecosystem category; and appropriately zoning the area and adopting corresponding ecological protection, restoration, and development measures. Hong Kong and Shenzhen are setting up permanent integrated observation points. They can be used as constant sample collection sites for studying the regional terrestrial vegetation coverage and changes in their ecological functions in suburban areas under rapid urbanization. Doing so will facilitate the protection of the ecosystem in the region. A study on cross-boundary greenways connection between Shenzhen and Hong Kong can also facilitate further work in this area.

Macau and Zhuhai

As an SAR of China, Macau, like Hong Kong, will become integrated into the PRD and in a larger sense, all of China. Today, borders still exist between Macau and Mainland China, as does a maritime border separating Macau from Hong Kong, which restrict flow of goods and ideas, and maintain differences among these three territories. The political change in the late 1990s has not necessarily changed the functions of the demarcation among these territories or even their business relationships with Taiwan. The changes were more dramatic in the late 1970s and 1980s than in the last decade. The borders today can be seen as legal constructs separating areas with different laws, physical and cultural landscapes with differing land uses and levels of wealth maintained through population and trade controls which allow some kinds of movement and exchange but prohibit others. The borders also maintain different cultures and psychologies. For non-Chinese visitors to Macau, the SAR remains a place where 'Portuguese culture' is a major attraction. The Macau SAR has gained new institutions, in the economic and trade field, which are geared towards the expansion of relations with Portuguese-speaking countries. On the other hand, in 1980 Zhuhai was approved as one of China's first five Special Economic Zones due to its location being adjacent to capitalist Macau. Zhuhai promptly became a boom town expanding from 100,000 inhabitants to become a modern city with a population of 1.9 million people in 2018. Despite this and certain signs that economic compatibility between Macau and its neighbours is not growing, Macau and Zhuhai are becoming a transborder metropolitan region and the delta has merged into one mutually dependent area (Statistical Bureau of Guangdong, 2018).

Economic integration

Zhuhai has important biopharmaceuticals, electrical appliances, manufacturing machinery, software, electronic information, and ocean-based industries. Zhuhai transportation is being transformed to further enhance Zhuhai's economic opportunities. Despite a small population of 1.9 million relative to the other eight cities in the PRD region, Zhuhai's 3.18 million overnight foreign tourist numbers in 2017 places Zhuhai third after Guangzhou and Shenzhen among the PRD cities. The important tourism sector is targeted for further expansion, focusing on leisure, sightseeing, and development of Hengqin into a tourist island targeting leisure travellers from across the globe (Statistical Bureau of Guangdong, 2018).

Hengqin is an island in Zhuhai, a prefecture-level city and SEZ in the Guangdong province of the People's Republic of China. Hengqin New Area is home to more than 7000 people among whom 4203 have been permanent residents since its establishment in 2009. Hengqin is a 106.46 km^2 coastal island tucked in the southern corner of the city of Zhuhai in Guangdong province. During a new round of reform and opening up policies in China, Hengqin has been targeted as an important area of land connecting the economies of Guangdong, Hong Kong, and Macau due to its geographical location being adjacent to Macau. Parts of Hengqin were leased to Macau by the State Council of the People's Republic of China starting in 2009 with the area expanding. In the leased parts of the island, Macau law applies. Hengqin Island is adjacent to the Taipa and Coloane Districts of Macau, with the Shisanmen Waterway separating them, and is connected to Macau's Cotai via the Lotus Bridge. The island is the largest among the 146 islands of Zhuhai, being roughly three times the size of Macau. It has broad bays, sandy beaches, strangely shaped jagged rocks, scenery, and natural vegetation cover (Zhuhai Hengqin New Area Administrative Committee, 2019).

Since the land reclamation and development, that Hengqin should be leased to Macau, which has very limited land and little room for further development, has been a growing opinion. By 1 September 2005, plans were revealed that the government of Guangdong would allow tax exemptions and adopt flexible immigration control in Hengqin to promote investment from Hong Kong and Macau. Banks in Macau can also provide cross-border mortgages to residents and enterprises of Hong Kong and vice versa when they buy property within the Hengqin development zone. Thus, Macau financial institutions can establish banks and joint ventures with Hong Kong financial institutions on Hengqin, strengthening Macau's relationship with Hong Kong. It was also disclosed that 126 Hong Kong and Macau financial enterprises have already registered in Hengqin until March 2018. With Hengqin island, the goal of the authorities is to create a combined Las Vegas and Orlando for Asia, with an expansive casino offering in Macau (see Figure 3.3), and at the same time non-gaming leisure and tourist activities. It helps promote Macau's 'moderate economic diversification via non-gaming elements and strengthened regional cooperation' by developing into a 'cultural and educational pilot zone and an international business, service, recreational and travel base' (Luo, 2018).

Figure 3.3 Wynn Macau.

Social integration

A more integrated and open GBA allows for the further development of these industries. For example, the completion of the aforementioned key infrastructure projects makes it easier for middle-class consumers to escape to Macau and Zhuhai for the weekend. The two main crossings between Macau and Zhuhai are located in Gongbei and Hengqin. The Gongbei crossing is open from 6:00 am to 1:00 am and this is where the majority of travellers' cross. Hengqin is open 24 hours and has the advantage of being located closer to the Cotai strip and Taipa, but entering on the Zhuhai side you are then faced with a long drive to the downtown area. With everything going on in Macau, it is easy to forget there is an entirely different city just across the border. For years, Zhuhai was just a cheap shopping destination for many Macau residents, but it has changed considerably. With a growing international population and regular infrastructure development, Zhuhai has opened more foreign restaurants, nightspots, and shopping options. Nevertheless, in many ways, it remains the sleepy seaside town it has always been, and it can be, a welcome escape from Macau's crowds.

Although the new wealth and prosperity have done many good things for Macau, questions about the social costs of gambling arise. Given that most of the gamblers come from China and Hong Kong, however, these costs are not likely to show up in Macau, but issues such as serious addiction in gambling do not disappear, and the costs must be borne somewhere. Another emerging issue resulting from Macau's new wealth is ensuring all citizens benefit from it. Improved social welfare programs and educational opportunities offer new prospects, but these must be comprehensive and sustained if they are to succeed. Macau's economy is prosperous, gambling is forbidden in mainland China, and the future for continued growth in gaming and Macau's related prosperity is promising. Other competitors have recently emerged in Singapore, Taiwan, the Philippines, and Korea, but Macau has established its reputation as the world's premier gaming centre, and its challengers can only marvel at its success (Luo & Lam, 2016; Luo, 2018; Luo & Lam, 2018).

On 27 June 2009, the government of Macau officially announced that the University of Macau would build its new campus on 1 km^2 of the island in a stretch directly facing the Cotai area, south of the current border post. This would be the first of other possible projects. Construction of the campus would take three years and would include an underwater tunnel. Macau law would apply in the university campus, and it would not be necessary to pass a formal border post. The Macau SAR will pay an amount of rent, which has not yet been set, for the use of the land. Professionals in Macau, such as engineers, doctors, and accountants, can also practice on Hengqin, thus providing more job opportunities for Macau residents and allowing for exchange in knowledge between the two administrative regions and China. Ultimately, these can help increase the overall education level within Macau.

Environmental integration

Zhuhai Airport is located 50 km southwest of the Zhuhai city. It is a modern airport with 11 million passengers in 2018. It directly connects the area with many Chinese cities, but it has no direct international destinations. To reach Zhuhai from outside China, one would usually fly to Macau, Hong Kong, Shenzhen or Guangzhou. All are within an hour or two of Zhuhai, with Macau and Hong Kong airports offering transport services direct to Zhuhai that do not require passing through Macau/Hong Kong passport/customs control. See the full details of each below.

Zhuhai Railway Station is located at the western end of Gongbei Port of Entry and Portas do Cerco at the border of Zhuhai and Macau (the world's busiest land border crossing). There are frequent HSR trains to Guangzhou and then beyond to/from Guilin, Beijing, Shanghai, Chengdu, and other main cities in China.

Zhuhai–Zhuhai Airport intercity railway, also known as the Zhuji intercity railway, is a regional rail in Zhuhai. It is part of PRD Metropolitan Region intercity railway system. Formerly, the railway was an extension of the Guangzhou–Zhuhai intercity railway.

The Hong Kong–Zhuhai–Macau Bridge (HZMB) is a mega-size sea crossing linking Hong Kong, Zhuhai, and Macau. It is the longest bridge-tunnel system sea-crossing in the world, crossing the waters of the Lingdingyang channel in the Pearl River Estuary. Hong Kong Port has a Passenger Clearance Building with a floor area of over 90,000 square metres and the 12 km Hong Kong Link Road connects the Hong Kong Port to the 29.6 km Main Bridge, which has a 22.9 km sea viaduct and 6.7 km sub-sea tunnel. After a distance of 41.6 km, the bridge arrives at the Zhuhai Port and Macau Port. From there, the 13.4 km Zhuhai Link Road brings the total length of the HZMB to 55 km. HZMB substantially cuts the travelling time between Hong Kong, Macau, and Zhuhai whilst further connecting Hong Kong to the major cities of the GBA and the cities of Guangxi province. Visitors can take buses connecting Hong Kong on one side and Zhuhai and Macau on the other whilst enjoying the view of the sea along the route (HZMB, 2019).

This bridge is the longest sea-crossing in the world and it connects the cities of Hong Kong, Zhuhai, and Macau. This crossing is open 24 hours (see Figure 3.4). The crossing connects to public transportation on Macau and Zhuhai. Long-distance connections on the Zhuhai side are available for various destinations in Guangdong province, including Guangzhou. The purpose of the bridge is to connect the Hong Kong SAR with Zhuhai in Guangdong Province, mainland China and Macau SAR. It primarily aims to ensure the flow of the travellers and commodities between Hong Kong, mainland China and Macau by establishing a mainland transport link between the eastern and western banks of the Pearl River. The building of the bridge would make the economic connection of the three sites closer and would contribute to the sustainable development of the territory. With such a dense transport system, the PRD area will become one of the great metropolitan regions in the world, with a degree of connectivity on par with Greater Tokyo, Greater Paris, and Greater London, but with faster trains and more modern facilities. This will help to integrate the numerous local industrial upgrading initiatives and greatly facilitate producer and consumer services. In the process, Hong Kong and Macau should join the PRD region in implementing its ambitious agenda and adjust their existing development trajectory accordingly.

Figure 3.4 The Hong Kong–Zhuhai–Macau Bridge.

Summary

Hong Kong is known as a world financial centre, Shenzhen is known as China's 'Silicon Valley' because of its innovation and start-up culture. Guangzhou is known for its manufacturing industry and as a logistics hub, and Macau and Zhuhai are known for leisure and tourism. Integrating the region's mainland cities with the two special administrative regions (Hong Kong and Macau) not only physically, but with coordinated and complementary laws and policies, is likely the plan's most controversial aspect. A more integrated GBA will help make businesses in the region more competitive as they will be more integrated into local and global supply chains. Businesses will also be able to increase their competitiveness by relocating to new development hotspots, such as Zhongshan, Zhaoqing, and Huizhou, where rent and labour costs are lower than Shenzhen and Guangzhou.

References

Altrock, U., & Schoon, S. (Eds). (2013). *Maturing megacities: The Pearl River delta in progressive transformation*. Dordrecht, NL: Springer Science & Business Media.

Brenner, N. (2004). *New state spaces: Urban governance and the rescaling of statehood*. New York: Oxford University Press.

Brenner, N. (2009). Open questions on state rescaling. *Cambridge Journal of Regions, Economy and Society*, 2, 123–139.

Camagni, R., & Capello, R. (2004). The city network paradigm: Theory and empirical evidence. *Contributions to Economic Analysis*, 266, 495–529.

Cooke, P. (2001). Regional innovation systems, clusters, and the knowledge economy. *Industrial and Corporate Change*, 10(4), 945–974.

Council, A. B. (2011). *Economic Transformation of the Greater Pearl River Delta: Moving Up the Value Chain*. Retrieved 20 October 2019, from www.asia businesscouncil.org/docs/PRDBriefing.pdf

Cox, K. R. (2009). 'Rescaling the state' in question. *Cambridge Journal of Regions, Economy and Society*, 2, 107–121.

Geddes, P. (1915). *Cities in evolution: An introduction to the town planning movement and to the study of civics*. London: Williams & Norgate.

Harrison, J. (2012). Life after regions? The evolution of city-regionalism in England. *Regional Studies*, 46, 1243e1259.

Harrison, J. (2014). The city-region: in retrospect, in snapshot, in prospect. In J. Harrison, & H. Michael (Eds), *Megaregions: Globalization's new urban form?*. Cheltenham: Edward Elgar.

Huang, Y. L., Li, F., Zheng, J. Q., & Li, F. (2006). Research about space structural system in tourism competitiveness around cites in the Pearl River Delta. *Geographic Research*, 25(4), 730–740.

HZMB. (2019). *Main Page*. Retrieved 10 October 2019 from www.hzmb.gov.hk/en/index.html

Klink, J. (2013). Development regimes, scales and state spatial restructuring: change and continuity in the production of urban space in metropolitan Rio de Janeiro, Brazil. *International Journal of Urban and Regional Research*, 37, 1168–1187.

Krätke, S., & Brandt, A. (2009). Knowledge networks as a regional development resource: A network analysis of the interlinks between scientific institutions and regional firms in the metropolitan region of Hanover, Germany. *European Planning Studies*, 17(1), 43–63.

Liang, M. Z. & Zhang, X. X. (2006). Study on tourism cooperation and tourism resource integration mode in Pan Pearl River Delta Region. *Economic Geographic*, 26(2), 335–339.

Liao, M. S., Dai, D. M. & Li, J. S. (2019, 20 June) *Hengqin will make every effort to build a demonstration zone for in-depth cooperation between Guangdong, Hong Kong and Macao*. Retrieved 10 October 2019 from http://zhuhaidaily.hizh.cn/html/2019-06/20/content_194579_1148881.htm

Luo, J. M. (2018). A measurement scale of corporate social responsibility in gambling industry. *Journal of Quality Assurance in Hospitality & Tourism*, 19(4), 460–475.

Luo, J. M., & Lam, C. (2016). *Corporate Social Responsibility and Responsible Gambling in Gaming Destination.* New York: Nova Science Publishers.

Luo, J. M., & Lam, C. F. (2018). *Entertainment Tourism.* Abingdon: Routledge.

Meijers, E. J. (2005). Polycentric urban regions and the quest for synergy: Is a network of cities more than the sum of the parts? *Urban Studies*, 42(4), 765–781.

Park, B.-G. (2013). State rescaling in non-Western contexts. *International Journal of Urban and Regional Research*, 37, 1115–1122.

Qianhai Media Center. (2019). *HK Entrepreneurs Chasing Dreams in Qianhai.* Retrieved 20 October 2019, from www.szqh.com.cn/What_is_Qianhai/News_Promotion_Event/201911/t20191106_18503146.htm

Statistical Bureau of Guangdong (2018). *Guangdong Statistical Yearbook.* China Statistics Press, Beijing.

Yeung, Y. M. (2010). The further integration of the Pearl River Delta: A new beginning of reform. *Environment and Urbanization Asia*, 1(1), 13–26.

Zhang, H. Q., Yan, Y. Q., & Lo, K. J. (2009). The facilitating and inhibiting factors in cooperative tourism development of the Greater Pearl River Delta (GPRD), China. *Journal of Quality Assurance in Hospitality & Tourism*, 10(2), 139–152.

Zhuhai Hengqin New Area Administrative Committee. (2019). *About Hengqin.* Retrieved 20 October 2019, from http://en.hengqin.gov.cn/Env/About/201503/02c67ca0f8204629a37a1305d9e442ea.shtml

4 The impact of city integration on tourism development

Travelling to city destinations has grown tremendously over the past decade, relative to the total international travel demand, and it has accounted for a rising share of overall travel demand aided by growing connectivity and rich cultural assets (WTTC, 2019). Spatial and social configuration of the cities were transformed along with the development and improvement of tourism and economy. These configurations demonstrated the transition of regional governance from territorial competition to regional coordination. City integration has positive and negative impacts on tourism development.

The positive effect of city integration on tourism development

New tourism product and multi destination travel

The GBA in the south of China is a newly developed area which combines different cultures. Regions in the GBA are usually modern and futuristic, but they also take pride in their traditions. In 1993, tourism departments from all regions in the GBA developed institutions to promote tourism, build long-term cooperation mechanisms, and explore different tourism areas. The 'one trip, multiple stop' is one of the products of the institutions. This product integrates tourism resources from three destinations aiming to combine the advantages of all destinations. In 2017, more than 10 tourism representatives coming from the GBA signed Guangdong–Hong Kong–Macau Bay Area Travel Trade Cooperation Summit. This summit includes four major aspects. The first aspect is to develop new tourism resources within the area and combine the advantages of all cities. The second is to enhance the 'one trip, multiple stop' tourism programme to develop a unique tourism product and promote tourism within the cities. The third is to create communication channels, daily contact mechanisms, a cooperation programme and an exchange programme. The fourth aspect is to enhance communication via irregular meeting and exchange visits (Liu, X, 2017).

The 'Outline Development Plan for the Guangdong–Hong Kong–Macau Greater Bay Area' was released in 2019. The outline clearly states that the Chinese government supports Hong Kong to become an international tourism hub and key demonstration area of 'one trip, multiple stop,' and to develop diverse tourism platform. The outline also states that to develop tourism in the GBA, one should enrich the number of travel boutique routes in the GBA. Tian (2019) also found that the Zhuhai–Hong Kong–Macau Bridge and the high-speed rail (HSR) are very important to the sales of tourism products. Since the opening of the bridge and the railways, group tours have increased to more than 150 per cent and tailormade tourism products have increased more than 300 per cent (Tian, 2019). This cooperation between Macau and Wanshan is an extension of Zhuhai's 'one-way, multi-station' tourism programme, which allows tourists to visit multiple destinations in one travel. This programme attracts domestic and international tourists who enjoy diversified products in one travel and increases the significance of the Zhuhai–Hong Kong–Macau Bridge (Kan & Li, 2018).

Caffyn and Lutz (1999) studied the method to combine attractions outside and inside the city centre. They successfully combined these attractions. The transportation system between these attractions are important because they allow tourists to access attractions outside the city centre and, hence, provide a mixture of tourism products. Building a transportation system and good infrastructure are inseparable with tourism development. Two major transportation infrastructures, Zhuhai–Hong Kong–Macau Bridge and the HSR, connects all cities in the GBA. These transportation infrastructures bring numerous opportunities to tourism providers to develop new tourism products. For example, during the Lunar Chinese New Year in 2019, many tourism providers in Guangdong provided 'one trip, multiple stops', which allows customers to visit Hong Kong, Macau, and Guangdong, all together in one trip. Since this package change, the traditional travel pattern goes from one trip and one stop, to one trip and multiple stops, therefore it is extremely popular. It does not only enrich people's travel experience with diversified cultural experience, but also allow people to further experience the GBA (Zhen, 2019).

Scale economies

The 9+2 cities in the GBA contribute to 13 per cent of China's GDP (Deloitte China, 2019).According to the China Centre for International

Economic Exchanges, the total economic output of the GBA will be similar to the economic output of the Tokyo Bay Area in 2020, and is expected to surpass the Tokyo Bay Area and the New York Bay Area in 2030. By then, the GBA will become the biggest bay area in the world. The estimated economic contribution of the GBA is around 30.4 trillion RMB (US$4.62 trillion) in 2030 (Hui, Li, Chen, & Lang, 2018).

The structural change of the industries in the GBA shows that coastal tourism has become one of the largest and most important industries in the world. For example, in 2013, the proportion of the primary, secondary, and tertiary industries that add value in the New York Bay Area is 0 per cent, 10.65 per cent, and 89.35 per cent, respectively, whereas coastal tourism is a crucial sector in tertiary industries. The contribution of the coastal tourism in San Francisco Bay Area is over 80 per cent (Zeng, 2018). In addition, the Gulf of Singapore relies heavily on tourism to earn foreign exchange. Therefore, to develop coastal tourism in the GBA, consolidating tourism resources and complementing each other with a solid foundation and a good relationship is necessary. In 2016, over 300 million tourists arrived in Guangdong, Hong Kong or Macau. Tourist spending increased from 265 billion RMB in 2005 to over 1 trillion RMB in 2017, which is an average growth equal to 12.6 per cent. Zeng (2018) believed that the Chinese government exert great attention and efforts to develop the GBA, which will bring enormous opportunities to the tourism industry.

The GBA is an important bay area economy in China. The effect of combining those cities is not one plus one. The unique feature of the GBA is its size. The population base of Guangzhou, Shenzhen, and Hong Kong is huge. There are many universities and talents in this area, which create scale effect and other potential advantages. Scale effect exists when there are interactions between elements and talents. The growth of R&D spending in China is enormous. The growth rate of R&D spending in the United States is around 2.5 per cent where China is over 10 per cent (Tang, 2018). Liu, Zhang, and Wu (2018) found that there is strategic significance of developing tourism in the GBA. They believe that tourism in the GBA represents a cluster effect, which is a necessary internal condition for the strategic development of the GBA and is useful to increase assimilation, interaction, economic connections and structures, and reduce internal cost. The total GDP increased from 8.17 trillion in 2014 RMB to 10.86 trillion RMB in 2018 (see Figure 4.1). The economic size exceeded that of Russia, which is the twelfth largest economy in the world (Yuan, 2018).

The assimilation between Guangzhou and Foshan will become the driving force of mass tourism in the city. Due to the development of the Internet, tourism in Guangzhou and Foshan will create synergy between tourism resources. Guangzhou and Foshan will then become the centre of

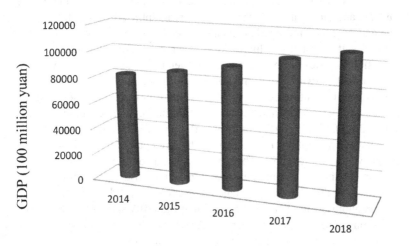

GDP in Guangdong-Hongkong-Macau Greater Bay Area

Figure 4.1 The GDP in the GBA increases consecutively from 2014 to 2018.

the development for economic tourism. These synergies will then spread to other surrounding areas and hence, create a city network effect (Guo, S, 2018).

On 5 March 2017, Premier Li Keqiang mentioned the 'Outline Development Plan of the Central Government and the State Council for the Guangdong–Hong Kong–Macau GBA'. This is the first time he mentioned it in an official government working report. This action shows that the development of the GBA has become a national issue. The Bay economy is an area or economic structure developed based on one or several bays or islands. This economic structure is extremely open, resources are efficiently allocated, elements are highly concentrated, and networks are highly developed. The major bay areas in the world are New York Bay Area, San Francisco Bay Area, Tokyo Bay Area, and Los Angeles Bay Area. Peng (2017) showed that the GBA and its surrounding cities exhibit a typical three-layer structure. The first layer is the core cities. The second layer is cities which are close to the core cities, such as Heyuan and Jieyang. The third layer is cities which are far away, such as Meizhou and Shantou. However, Peng (2017) also argued that the GBA network relies heavily on Hong Kong and Shenzhen as the medium and centre to spread the synergetic effect and does not have a reasonable structure of layers.

The Bay Area economy is defined as cities and area surrounding the bay area and these cities use their coastal geographic advantage to consolidate and integrate into a unique area or economy system with international influence. It is usually a highly open economy with efficient resources allocation abilities, with a strong spill over effect and highly developed international network. It is the carrier of future industrial upgrade; the improvement of future economy, society, environment, and resources; the change of city structure and the carrier of further regional economy (Zhang & Gu, 2017). 'Optimum Currency Area', pioneered by Robert Mundell, is a theory which explains the conditions that are optimal to form a common currency among the region. The advantages of a common currency include a common finance and market, low transaction cost, increased trade and product mobility. These advantages help create a solid foundation of an open economy. Liu, T. (2017) argued that the GBA satisfied many of the conditions of the 'Optimum Currency Area', which means the GBA should gradually integrate into an area with a single currency.

Branding effect

In December 2017, tourism providers from Guangzhou, Hong Kong, and Macau approved the Articles of the Tourism Federation of Cities in Guangdong, Hong Kong, and Macau. The articles adhere to 'cooperative development, brand creation, and market sharing' and aims to consolidate resources, joint marketing, and brand creation to enhance the cooperation between tourism providers in the GBA and develop the GBA to internationally recognized bay area and tourism destination. According to the Annual Tourism Working Report (2018), the next step of the GBA is to develop an integrated brand, an integrated coordination and development mechanism, and organize the development plan of all cities within the GBA. This will be key to the future development of the GBA (Ding, 2018).

Tourism providers in Guangdong, Hong Kong, and Macau have complemented their advantages and have promoted regional tourism brand since 1993 by forming marketing institutions in the three destinations. For example, in February 2018, the Macau Tourism Board, Hong Kong Tourism Board, and the Guangdong Tourism Board formed a mutual agreement to enhance oversea promotion by utilizing existing tourism cooperation mechanism (Zhan & Zhou, 2018) and increasing sales and spill over effect of the cultural brand of the GBA (Zhuang, Wu, & Zhou, 2019).

Combining the realistic foundations and conditions of Guangdong–Hong Kong–Macau GBA, strengthening the city brand construction in

GBA, it is conducive to deepen exchanges and cooperation between the mainland and Hong Kong and Macau, achieve mutual benefit and win–win. Also, to inject new energy into the development of Hong Kong and Macau, and enhance the competitiveness of the cities of Bay Area. The strategy of the GBA is to incorporate tourism into the branding of the city. The strategy will bring more cultural connotations, promote the brand of the city and advertise travelling in the city simultaneously. In addition, this strategy will increase the influence and popularity of the cities and further promote the social development and the economic construction of the GBA (Zhao, 2018).

Balance regional development

The GBA experienced periods when cities were developed individually and separately. Cities in the GBA began their cooperation by having Hong Kong and Macau as the front door sales and the PRD as the factory of the products. This cooperation is unofficial and unorganized. Nowadays, cooperation and coordination between cities in the GBA are tighter, proactive and interconnected from production, life and policy perspectives. Guangzhou and Shenzhen are growing quickly during the last decade. The gap between Guangzhou, Shenzhen and Hong Kong are narrower (Zhou, Deng, & Shi, 2018) (see Figure 4.2).

Different cities in the GBA have different tourism economic development level. Figure 4.1 and 4.2 show the tourism revenue and tourist arrival

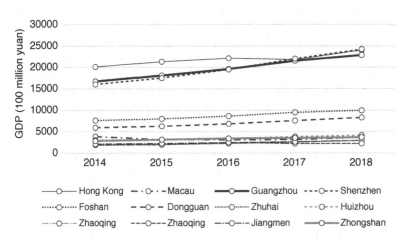

Figure 4.2 GDP of each city in Guangdong–Hong Kong–Macau Greater Bay Area from 2014 to 2018.

in all cities in the GBA. First, the economic tourism development in Guangdong is unbalanced. The northern, eastern and western regions have lower economic tourism development than the PRD. Second, the total tourism economy of Guangdong is behind those of Hong Kong and Macau. These results are mainly caused by the lack of public service level in the tourism sector and tourism infrastructures. During the development of the GBA and the 'One Belt, One Road' initiative, Shenzhen and Hong Kong will become the driver of economic tourism development in the region and extend their influence to enhance the economic tourism development in Huizhou and Dongguan proactively. The combination of the free trade zone in Macau and Zhuhai will enhance the development of tourism, leisure, distinctive towns, and environment (Zhuang, Wu, & Zhou, 2019). The governments in the GBA should increase the mobility in the area via tourism, which means encouraging people to travel around the GBA. This policy is beneficial to the economic development of the area and increase the assimilation of the people in Hong Kong and Macau to the national plan (Liu & Li, 2019).

The 'Outline Development Plan for the Guangdong–Hong Kong–Macau Greater Bay Area' reduces the constraints between the three regions such that they can complement their advantages, coordinate their resources and share their markets. Therefore, the culture in the GBA will have a more systematic, balanced, and open development (Qi, Li, & Wang, 2019). Under the structure of the GBA, many bridges connecting Hong Kong, Macau, and China are built. For example, alongside the Hong Kong–Macau–Zhuhai Bridge, Nansha Bridge began to operate in April 2019. Over 70 million people in the GBA can travel efficiently. The growth of tourism is expected to increase dramatically (Song, 2019).

Goh, Li, and Zhang (2015) found that when tourism demand and supply across regions converge, economic development across regions reduces. In addition, they found that domestic tourism development is a relatively more important variable than international tourism development to reduce regional economic imbalance. Li, Goh, Qiu, and Meng (2014) found that the regional disparity in China mainly exists between the coastal region and the inland region. However, disparity within the same region is relatively small. The authors also concluded that domestic tourism could help increase the economic development at the regional level.

Complement tourism resources

Ever since the 'Open Door Policy' in 1979, industrialization and urbanization have created agglomeration effect. However, urbanization and industrialization are not without costs or negative effects. These costs and negative effects eventually decrease the living standard of citizens. Besides, when citizens in the urban area demand the opportunities of leisure, recreation, and vacation activities, sub-urban areas will be developed, showing the trend of 'the counter urbanization'. As the HSR and highway network between Hong Kong, Macau, and Guangdong are fully developed, this network leads to not only a flow of investments, but also tourists. This flow of tourists eventually shapes the spatial pattern of tourism. From urban tourism and recreation area in the GBA, to leisure agriculture and rural tourism belt in urban suburb, ecological tourism and recreational belt in the mountainous area of northern Guangdong and coastal tourism and recreational belt in Southern Guangdong, even to leisure and recreational belt to experience regional customs in provincial boundaries, these four levels are distributed just like fan, echelon, and ribbon. These recreational belts become places where citizens in the urban area travel to during the weekends. These recreational activities will increase the living standard of the citizens and enhance the level of integration of the GBA, as well as the urban and rural area (Liu, Zhang, & Wu, 2018). Furthermore, different cities in the GBA exhibit different characteristics. For example, Macau is famous for its gaming business, Hong Kong is famous for its shopping hubs and Zhuhai is famous for its health tourism. In the future, the development of the GBA will help support the resources of each city and will increase the attractiveness of the GBA as single tourism destination (Tao, 2019).

Capital investment to tourism industry

Upon completion of EU integration, the number of tourists visiting Turkey will increase in terms of quality and quantity. Foreign capital investment in tourism will increase, and the resources for the infrastructure investment for tourism sector will increase thanks to utilization of structural funds (Cengiz, Eryilmaz, & Eryilmaz, 2006).

Hong Kong is undoubtedly a part of China. However, Hong Kong possesses completely different economic, legal, and social systems. Seeing that Hong Kong is an international financial centre, it can utilize its international network and expertise to bring foreign investments to China. Nevertheless, Hong Kong can develop an international market with companies in China and, hence, achieve economic development. For example, as RMB becomes the common currency within the GBA, cross-boundary investments will abound between Hong Kong and China, which will increase the investment opportunities available to people from both areas. For the tourism industry, the Outline Development Plan sets out to 'deepen cooperation among Guangdong, Hong Kong and Macau in the cultural and creative industries, and progressively open up the market'. Specifically, the plan intends to promote cooperation among the film and television industries in Guangdong, Hong Kong, and Macau; strengthen film investment and cooperation and exchanges among talents and support tourism development.

Increase tourist arrival

The development of the GBA will also increase the number of tourist arrivals. The San Francisco Bay Area is a classic example of such an effect. Qu and Im (2002) found that the number of tourists from Southeast Asia escalated from 2.1 million in 1990 to 3.3 million in 1996. The San Francisco Bay Area is also a main transportation hub for people travelling to the United States. The meaning of the GBA for tourism is that GBA creates a massive concentrated tourism market. Guangdong, Hong Kong, and Macau possess huge tourism markets, regardless of the terms of tourism demand or supply. This tourism demand and supply represents a huge power consumption. The development of the GBA can provide protection and momentum towards tourism development (Tao, 2019).

Following the opening of the Hong Kong–Macau–Zhuhai Bridge, the travel distance between Zhuhai and Hong Kong International Airport curtailed from 200 km to 40 km. The travelling time is reduced from four hours to only 45 minutes. This attracts not only more international tourists to Zhuhai through Hong Kong and Macau, but also Chinese tourists to travel to Hong Kong and Macau through Zhuhai. In 2016, there were nearly five million international tourists who travelled to Zhuhai. Among which, over three million tourists spent at least one night in Zhuhai. In addition, domestic tourists who travelled to Zhuhai reached 34 million. More than half of these domestic tourists sojourned at least one night in Zhuhai (Chen & Peng, 2018).

The negative effect of city integration on tourism development

Tourism product similarity

Although the development of the GBA will highly benefit tourism, it also entails several disadvantages. With the exception of Jiangmen, many cities in the PRD have similar cultures and characteristics. Despite abundant tourism resources in the GBA, it remains to lack a core element, such as Li Jiang in Guilin (Zhou, 2018). Liu, Zhang, and Wu (2018) also discovered that the level of complementariness between Hong Kong, Macau, and Zhuhai decreases when the competition increases. There are pressures to enhance the co-operation between cities. For example, the four main cruise ports in the GBA are geographically adjacent to one another. In particular, the tourism products offered by Namsha Port and Shekou Cruise Center are highly similar, which results in an increase of competition (Zhou & Wu, 2018).

Tourism carrying capacity (overcrowding)

Some researchers began studying the carrying capacity in the 1930s, but many researches in this area sprung in the 1960s. Although carrying capacity can be considered a part of sustainable tourism, it has recently become less popular. The assessment of the carrying capacity of a destination requires one to consider the capacity of the tourism facilities and infrastructures and the surrounding ecological setting and resources. Because the number of tourists in Hong Kong have recently tremendously increased, the carrying capacity of Hong Kong becomes a crucial matter. Many people argued that the increase in tourists has already exceeded the carrying capacity of Hong Kong, which has resulted in some negative behaviour toward tourists. Others claimed that Hong Kong is a free and open society, so the entry of tourists need not be prohibited. Therefore, the government should increase the carrying capacity of Hong Kong to accommodate the rising number of tourist's arrival (Liu, Zhang, & Wu, 2018).

Russo (2002) described the above situation by a vicious cycle. Despite the numerous tourist attractions in the city and increasing number of people compelled to be excursionists, people are less likely to stay overnight when the city is overcrowded, thus less time to explore the city. They will be unable to provide revenues, such as those from hotel accommodations, to the city; instead, they would try to compress all sightseeing attractions into one day. Therefore, many people will visit the same attraction simultaneously because there is a logical sequence of visiting, based on the location of the attractions. This behaviour will exacerbate the existing overcrowding situations in those attractions. As a result, people will have less intention to stay in the city overnight, creating the vicious cycle.

This economic, social, and demographic transition has resulted in new challenges facing the GBA, such as over-urbanization, increasing densities, internal migration, overcrowding, and the rising cost of living partly fuelled by speculative development and floating population due to migrant workers. Many existing cities that adopted smart technologies suffer from the same critical urban challenges, such as urbanization through migration, infrastructure development and mobility issues due to traffic congestions, car-oriented development, poor accessibility and walkability, lack of high quality public space with landscaped green spaces, higher densities with overcrowding and poorer quality of life (Govada & Rodgers, 2019).

Authenticity of visitor experiences

As for the impact of urbanization on the authenticity of visitor experiences (Stephen & Keith, 2019), the basis of the criterion of 'authenticity' would require more than the concept of collective memory to justify its use. Heynen (2006) argued that practical problems may emerge when one maintains the authenticity of a rebuilt heritage. For example, many rebuilt heritages fail to restore the original authentic themes, and this can be attributed to the questionable rebuilding implemented. Tourism reduces the authenticity of traditional cultural events, the commodifying effects of tourism downgrading local culture to a series of inauthentic events produced solely for tourist consumption, depreciating their meaning and relevance for local people (Richards & Greg, 2007).

If a remote destination develops, then it modernizes and becomes more like the tourist's society. Less different and distinct, and no longer 'primitive', it loses its appeal. As cultural assets are refined as consumables for tourists, culture becomes commoditized. The destination appears less authentic, so the value of the product is reduced (Cole, 2007). City planners, when deciding the policy, should be aware of the authenticity and preserve authenticity of the tourist resources, such as the heritage rebuilding and urban re-infrastructure.

Summary

The GBA will strive to become a world tourism destination through cross-region tourism within the area. Through cross-region tourism, the GBA will become a world tourism-friendly area with the investment amounting to 10 trillion RMB in 10 tourism sectors, such as health and leisure, marine, urban, culture and creation, agricultural and education, and research tourism. However, the integration of the cities in the GBA entails positive and negative impact on tourism sector, therefore, city planners or tourism policy makers should minimize the negative effects of the integration.

References

Caffyn, A., & Lutz, J. (1999). Developing the heritage tourism product in multi-ethnic cities. *Tourism Management*, 20(2), 213–221.
Cengiz, H., Eryilmaz, S., & Eryilmaz, Y. (2006). The Importance of Cultural Tourism in the EU Integration Process. Retrieved 25 September 2019, from http://citeseerx.ist.psu.edu/viewdoc/download?doi=10.1.1.614.568&rep=rep1&type=pdf

Chen, X. L., & Peng, M. L. (2018). Research on Zhuhai's Slow Tourism Development Strategy Based on Sharing Economy. *Contemporary Economics*, 13, 81–83.

Cole, S. (2007). Beyond authenticity and commodification. *Annals of Tourism Research*, 34(4), 943–960.

Deloitte China (2019). Decoding the Outline Development Plan for Guangdong–Hong Kong–Macao Greater Bay Area (GBA). [Online]. Retrieved 1 February 2020, from www2.deloitte.com/content/dam/Deloitte/cn/Documents/international-business-support/deloitte-cn-csg-decoding-greater-bay-area-plan-en-190415.pdf

Ding, Chi (2018, June). Exploring the multi destination travel tourism market in Guangdong–Hong Kong–Macao Greater Bay Area. *Time Weekly*. Retrieved 25 September 2019, from www.time-weekly.com/html/20180619/251765_1.html

Goh, C., Li, H., & Zhang, Q. (2015). Achieving balanced regional development in China: Is domestic or international tourism more efficacious? *Tourism Economics*, 21(2), 369–386.

Govada, S. S., & Rodgers, T. (2019). Towards smarter regional development of Hong Kong within the Greater Bay Area. In T. M. Vinod Kumar (ed.), *Advances in 21st Century Human Settlements* (pp. 101–171). Springer Nature Singapore Pte Ltd.

Guo, S. P. (2018). The development of Guangdong–Hong Kong–Macao Greater Bay Area bring new opportunities. Retrieved 28 September 2019, from http://news.10jqka.com.cn/20180430/c604195851.shtml

Guo, X. X. (2018). Study on The Development of Tourism Economy in Guangdong, Hong Kong, Macao and Great Bay Area. *Taxation and Economy*, 2(217), 19–25.

Heynen, H. (2006). Questioning authenticity. *National Identities*, 8(3), 287–300.

Hui, C. M., Li, X., Chen, T. T., & Lang, W. (2018). Deciphering the spatial structure of China's megacity region: A new bay area – The Guangdong-Hong Kong-Macao Greater Bay Area in the making. *Cities*, in press. https://doi.org/10.1016/j.cities.2018.10.011

Kan, X. L., & Li, H. (2018). Study on Tourism Cooperation between Zhuhai Island and Macao in the Times of Greater Bay Area of Guangdong, Hong Kong and Macao. *Advances in Social Science, Education and Humanities Research*, 233, 1061–1064.

Li, H. Y., Goh, C., Qiu, H. Z., & Meng, F. (2014). Effect of Tourism on Balanced Regional Development: A Dynamic Panel Data Analysis in Coastal and Inland China. *Asia Pacific Journal of Tourism Research*, 2(35), 37–41.

Liu, M., Zhang, Q. Q., & Wu, Y. (2018, June). A Summary of Studies on the Problems of Guangdong–Hong Kong–Macao Greater Bay Area. *National Governance Weekly*. Retrieved 28 September 2019, from www.rmlt.com.cn/2018/0611/520686.shtml?from=singlemessage

Liu, T. (2017). Comparison between Guangdong–Hong Kong–Macao Greater Bay Area and Foreign Major Bay Areas and Other Domestic City Clusters: A Perspective from Major Component Analysis. *Hong Kong and Macao Research*, 4, 61–94.

Liu, X. T. (2017). Tourism development in Guangdong–Hong Kong–Macao Greater Bay Area welcomes new opportunities. Retrieved 28 September 2019, from http://news.163.com/17/1222/08/D68DS71D00014AEE.html

Liu, Y. Y., & Li, Y. F. (2019). Tourism Development in Guangdong–Hong Kong–Macao Greater Bay Area bring new opportunities. Retrieved 28 September 2019, from http://2www.rmzxb.com.cn/c/2019-04-12/2328085_3.shtml

Peng, M. F. (2017). Economic Spatial Connection and Spatial Structure of Guangdong–Hong Kong–Macao Greater Bay and the Surrounding Area Cities – An Empirical Analysis Based on Improved Gravity Model and Social Network Analysis. *Economic Geography*, 37(12), 57–64.

Qi, Y. M., Li, X. F., & Wang, S. W. (2019). The development plan for Guangdong–Hong Kong–Macao Greater Bay Area, what new opportunities will be welcomed in the cultural development of the Bay Area. Retrieved 28 September 2019, from https://new.qq.com/omn/20190220/20190220A13JVI.html

Qu, H., & Im, H. J. H. (2002). A study of Southeast Asia tourists' perceptions of service quality in the San Francisco bay area. *Journal of Travel & Tourism Marketing*, 13(3), 35–60.

Richards, & Greg. (2007). Culture and authenticity in a traditional event: the views of producers, residents, and visitors in Barcelona. *Event Management*, 11(1), 33–44.

Russo, A P. (2002). The 'Vicious Circle' of tourism development in heritage cities. *Annals Tourism Research*, 29 (1), 165–182.

Song, D. (2019). 12 major trends of tourism development in Guangdong–Hong Kong–Macao Greater Bay Area. Retrieved 28 September 2019, from www.sohu.com/a/321065364_100134321

Stephen, F. M. & Keith, B. (2019). *A research agenda for sustainable tourism*. Cheltenham: Edward Elgar

Tang, Z. T. (2018, September). The scale economies effect has been formed in Guangdong–Hong Kong–Macao Greater Bay Area. *Nanfang Daily*. Retrieved 28 September 2019, from http://dy.163.com/v2/article/detail/DSULT-L3V0550037C.html

Tao, N. N. (2019). The planning of Guangdong–Hong Kong–Macao Greater Bay Area mentioned tourism 46 times. Retrieved 28 September 2019, from www.thepaper.cn/newsDetail_forward_3014563

Tian, H. (2019). Building a world-class destination is the 'new power' for the development of the cultural tourism industry in Guangdong–Hong Kong–Macao Greater Bay Area. Retrieved 28 September 2019, from http://travel.people.com.cn/n1/2019/0222/c41570-30897670.html

WTTC. (2019). *City Travel & Tourism Impact 2018*. Retrieved 28 September 2019, from www.wttc.org/-/media/files/reports/economic-impact-research/cities-2018/city-travel-tourism-impact-2018final.pdf

Yuan, J. (2018). *Annual Report of Guangdong, Hong Kong and Macau Bay Area Construction (2018)*. Beijing: Social Sciences Academic Press.

Zeng, L. (2018). Study on the efficiency and the cooperative direction of tourism and leisure industry in Guangdong–Hong Kong–Macao Greater Bay Area. *Open Journal of Social Sciences*, 06(1), 93–105.

Zhang, R. X., & Gu, Z. T. (2017). The origin and next move of Guangdong–Hong Kong–Macao Greater Bay. *Reform*, 279(5), 64–73.

Zhao, C. Y. (2018). Research on the 'Implanted' Model of Tourism Advertising in City Brand Promotion under the Strategy of Guangdong–Hong Kong–Macao Greater Bay Area. *Advances in Economics, Business and Management Research*, 68, 687–689.

Zhen, H. M. (2019). Multi destination travel products are popular. Retrieved 1 October 2019, from https://file.ccmapp.cn/group1/M00/00/52/rApntVyJwcCAZ wtvAAAe0bMMGmc86.html

Zhou, C. S., & Deng, H. H. Shi, C. Y. (2018). A Study on Synergic Development of Guangdong–Hong Kong–Macao Greater Bay Area. *Planners*, 4(34), 5–12.

Zhou, R. G. (2018, December). How to solve the dilemma of the inbound tour in Guangdong–Hong Kong–Macao Greater Bay Area? *Nanfang Daily*. Retrieved 1 October 2019, from www.sohu.com/a/285522133_100116740

Zhou, Z. Y., & Wu, R. J. (2018, June). The problem of the competition of the cruise industry in Guangdong–Hong Kong–Macao Greater Bay Area. *21st Century Business Herald*. Retrieved 2 October 2019, from http://epaper.21jingji. com/html/2018-06/05/content_87421.htm

Zhuang, W. G., Wu, W. X., & Zhou, K. M. (2019). High-quality tourism cooperation in Guangdong–Hong Kong–Macao Greater Bay Area. Retrieved 2 October 2019, from www.gdass.gov.cn/messageinfo_7566.shtml

5 Trends and issues of city integration and tourism

The future of city integration in China

Mega-urban city clusters trends

During urbanization, some cities eventually grow into metropolitan areas. Other cities form a complex, functional, regional entity and transform into a mega region. The building of a mega region requires a structured urban system, which describes the structure and interaction within the region. The definition of mega region should be carefully defined given that a mega region can be one single mega metropolitan area or a group of several. A mega region is a sector of dynamic entities linked with economic, infrastructural, and technological processes. According to Rodrigue, Comtois, and Slack (2017), a mega region can be defined in three ways.

Metropolitan Area. A metropolitan area is a large city that is officially defined as a jurisdictional unit with fully functioning labour, consumption, and production market. It is the building block of the international economy. A metropolitan area does not necessarily have to be a continuous connected urban area. Rural areas can also be a part of a metropolitan area. In addition, it does not have to follow a single jurisdiction. However, the transportation system in the metropolitan area connects all the cities within the area.

Extended Metropolitan Region (EMR). EMR is a large urban agglomerate combined with a network of secondary or satellite cities. Within an EMR, there are many infrastructures, such as agricultural activities, large-scale real estate, and industrial areas. Rural areas are usually included in the region.

Mega-Urban Region (MUR). A MUR typically comprises several metropolitan areas, which some can be EMRs. Areas in a MUR are connected through an efficient transportation system. Despite physical connections, areas in a MUR are also connected socially and economically. Since MURs can span over several hundreds of kilometres, the population in MURs is huge. Although there is no official or formal definition of the size of MUR, the population in MURs is usually over 10 million and these people are generally located in the EMRs within the region. MUR is a specialized and interdependent region with a comprehensive system of production, consumption, and distribution which connects the world, the region and other smaller areas in the nation.

According to the estimate of McKinsey & Company (2011), roughly 40 MURs exist in the world. The total population in these MURs is over 1 billion. The most crucial urban regions in the world are Yangtze River Delta, the Takaido Corridor, and the PRD, which are all located in Asia. The population of the Yangtze River Delta, the Takaido Corridor, and the PRD are 88, 80, and 70 million, respectively. These regions are the largest accumulation of urban infrastructure globally. Other examples of MURs are Rhine/Scheldt Delta, which is a MUR combined by cities in Belgium, Netherlands, and Germany, and Kuala Lumpur in Singapore. Given that the United States is one of the biggest countries in the world, there are several MURs in the U.S. For example, BostWash between Boston and Washington contains 44 million people and ChiPitts between Chicago and Pittsburgh contains 54 million people. Although ChiPitts contains a slightly larger population, it is less integrated and more slatternly located (McKinsey & Company, 2011).

Urbanization and industrialization are the key driving forces of the extraordinary growth of China in recent decades. Since the Open Door Policy in 1978, many people in China escaped from poverty. The urbanization level in China increased from 19 per cent in 1978 to around 60 per cent in 2018. During this period, many cities became mega cities and even clustered with MURs. Bei–Shang–Guang is a classic example. The development of the special economic zones creates numerous job opportunities and attract FDI. People from the rural areas moved to the cities for better jobs. The interaction between these economic policies, investments, and people in the cities create the MUR (UBS, 2018).

A MUR is potentially the future driving force of sustainable urbanization and economic development in China. There are 19 city clusters that are mentioned in the thirteenth Five-Year Plan and these clusters are attracting many people. To efficiently manage these people, the Chinese government should increase co-ordination between local governments within the clusters. This will not only entail social and economic benefits, but also sustainability benefits. When cities within the clusters become more integrated, productivity increases. This will not only increase the income of the people, but also fulfil the national policy goal of increasing domestic consumption. MURs across the world may learn from China's experience. As the world grows more urbanized, MURs also become more interconnected even when they are from different countries. Therefore, city clusters self-select themselves into high-performance and well-connected urban area and slow, rural and remote area.

Smart cities in China

Smart city has many definitions. From a general perspective, a smart city is defined as a city, which is sustainable and liveable. Alternatively, Harrison et al. (2010) defined a smart city as a city, which is instrumental, interconnected, and intelligent. Lee, Phaal and Lee (2013)described it as a city, which utilizes recent technologies, such as information and communication technologies. Barrionuevo, Berrone, and Ricart (2012) provided a similar definition, but the authors added that these technologies and resources should be co-ordinated in a method to integrate the urban centre in a sustainable and habitable manner. Chen (2012) provided an example in which these new technologies, especially communication and sensor technologies, can be integrated into the cities' infrastructures to enhance electrical, transportation, and other logistical operation. Ultimately, these technologies will improve people's living standard. More specifically, Giffinger, Fertner, Kramar, Kalasek, Pichler-Milanović, and Meijers (2007) identified six key elements to define a smart city. These elements are smart people, smart economy, smart environment, smart governance, smart living, and smart mobility. The restructuring and building of cities are complex issues with many challenges, such as resilience against climate change and natural disasters. Air pollution is an emerging environmental issue in China (He, Huo, & Zhang, 2002). When smart cities are being constructed, many key facilities, such as cleaner energy technologies, advanced transportation methods, new water systems, and innovative construction methods improve people's living standard. In addition, smart cities can utilize information technologies to improve the quality of city operations and services.

New technologies also provide an alternative way to affect and transform the city to become more sustainable, environmentally friendly, convenient, and accessible. These objectives or outcomes are dependent on each other and pursuing these objectives simultaneously by integrative solutions leads will create more viable city. For example, when transportation systems in the city become efficient or autonomous, vehicles become more available, and the demand for parking space and road use will reduce. The extra space can be used to build other recreational facilities, such as playgrounds or bike lanes, or to reduce the density of buildings and provide more housing and hence reduce the housing prices.

Technologies enhance the living standards of people and affect the behaviours of people. Mobile technologies increase the connectivity between service providers and end users. This increase of connectivity makes the interaction tighter, faster, more personal, and more comprehensive. For example, the emergence of a sharing economy allows people to share their physical assets, such as vehicles or apartments with others in exchange for a fee. Mapping technologies applicable to cities to actual urban challenges requires moving from science-based research and development, to human-focused use cases. Many resilience problems, such as health, transportation, sanitation, public safety, economic development, sustainability, and street maintenance can be resolved by sensors or real-time data. ICTs and proliferation of sensor through Internet of Things are novel technologies that offer new ways to manage and develop cities. Governments are exploring new data and analytics technologies and conducting pilot tests to improve their services.

The concept of smart city is not new. Many cities, such as Hong Kong, Shenzhen, Guangzhou, and Macau have initialized the smart city initiatives (Hong Kong 2030+, 2017). Given that the GBA combines the '9+2 cities' into one mega/meta area, the concept of smart cities can be applied to a regional level. However, to apply a smart city in a regional level, the application of technologies alone is insufficient. The co-operation and interaction between cities and the mobility of people, infrastructure qualities, network of transportation, environmental protection, education, health care, awareness, and social cohesion should be carefully designed. The design of these components will positively and significantly affect the region.

Issues relative of city integration to tourism

High-speed transportation

Transportation allows people to enjoy different activities, such as leisure, shopping, working, and education. Therefore, modern transportation system is built based on this objective aiming to connect different regions based on infrastructure and urban form (Gandy, 2003; Addie, 2013). HSR, which is defined as rail system with an average speed of over 200 km/h, is a recent transportation method employed in many countries (Chen, 2012; Levinson, 2012). HSR is a new form of sustainable transportation system. Railroads enable people to travel and allow the economic activities between different regions to connect, so developing railroads is important to economic development. Hence, since China holds the second largest railroad system in the world it is reasonable. In addition, China is building the largest HSR, which will improve connectivity and reduce the travelling time between cities. The HSR in China will extend its reach to small urban areas and ultimately will reach every city with a population over 500,000. As more rails are developed, the number of people boarding the HSR will increase simultaneously. The connection between the first and second tier cities in China also provides new economic opportunities to these cities. Before the HSR, travelling from Shanghai to Hangzhou, would take four hours. However, with HSR, the travel time with same distance is curtailed to less than an hour. This is one example out of many where cities are connected more efficiently by HSR. The HSR to Hong Kong began construction in 2000. The HSR in Hong Kong is called Guangzhou–Shenzhen–Hong Kong Express Rail Link, which is 26 km in length and runs from West Kowloon to the Shenzhen/Hong Kong boundary (see Figure 5.1). This is also the fastest cross-boundary land transport in Hong Kong, connecting Hong Kong to 58 mainland stations without interchanging (MTR, 2019).

The introduction of HSRs provides an alternative travel method to those who prefer transportation by land. Despite that China possesses the fastest HSR technology in the world, China Aerospace Science and Industry Corporation is developing a 'high-speed flying train', a new train, which uses

Figure 5.1 Guangzhou–Shenzhen–Hong Kong Express Rail Link.

passenger pod, a near-vacuum tube and magnetic levitation. The top speed reaches 2485 miles per hour or 4000 km per hour and is 10 times faster than the current HSR, four times faster than commercial flights and three times faster than sound. Although no one knows when the 'high-speed flying train' will become available to public, through development, more than 200 patents are created. These patents and new technologies will eventually be integrated to the One Belt, One Road initiative.

Smart tourism destinations

As more smart cities are developed, smart tourism destination, which a tourism product whose destinations are smart cities, is developed correspondingly (Buhalis, 2000). The characteristics of smart city, such as innovation, technology, sustainability, and accessibility not only increase the living standards of their citizens, but also increase the appeal towards tourists. These characteristics become important factors when tourists are making their travel decisions, becoming known as smart tourism destinations. Smart tourism destinations focus on the combination of ICT and social culture to fulfil the needs of tourists. (Huang, Yuan, & Shi, 2012). By incorporating new technologies to tourists, smart cities, and smart city destinations can enhance tourism experience and attract more tourists (Ritchie & Crouch, 2003). Cohen (2012) further explained that smart city destinations can install more tourism applications to provide wider and unrestricted access to information through an effectively monitored platform.

There are nearly 1000 smart cities in the world, and roughly half of them are in China. Anderlini (2019) reported that the Chinese government expects around 500 billion RMB will be invested in the smart cities by public or private investment. These investments can improve the technological innovation in the cities in various aspects. For instance, people in Yinchuan use facial recognition to pay for buses. Some areas in China installed intelligent lockers, which allows packages to be delivered even when people are not at home. In addition, the rubbish bins in some areas will send an automatic message to garbage collectors when they are full, which reduces the chance and duration of a full garbage bin (UBS, 2018).

Although some people prefer to travel out of town to enjoy moments away from modern technologies, many people prefer to stay connected with modern conveniences, such as social media and running water. These technologies also include access to electronic payments, online maps and GPS, and finding nearby restaurants with reviews. To cater to this preference, governments in many destinations apply these technologies to the tourism industry and transform their cities into smart cities. These innovations not only invite more tourists, they also improve the tourism industry and labour market.

To ensure the tourism industry is keeping up with the development of technologies, tourism authorities develop new initiatives. The Five-Year Plan on smart tourism by the China National Tourism Administration in which all top-rated scenic locales will allow online reservations by 2020. At the same time, tourists can enjoy electronic tour guides and free Wi-Fi. To increase the level of security, major transportation methods, such as tour buses, cruise and scenic spots, will have real-time monitoring systems. In addition, some smart hotels will allow people to check in using their mobile phones. Furthermore, many international tourists tend to research the destination before they travel, however traditional tourism providers in China fail to recognize the importance of their online image. These new technologies will allow authorities to collect more travel preferences and will improve tourists' experience. Different types of tourists, such as family tour, free independent traveller(FIT) and high-end tourists, will be captivated by the unique experience.

Summary

This chapter describes the new form of city integration and discusses the trend in tourism development. The terms 'smart cities' and 'smart tourism destinations' have become extremely popular in the recent decade. Smart tourism destinations are smart cities that utilize information technology and innovations to enable enjoyment and experiences for tourists. This chapter focuses on the linkages between smart cities and smart tourism destinations. It helps understand and execute sustainable plans for the development of smart cities, which will ultimately pave the way towards smart tourism destinations.

References

Addie, J. P. D. (2013). Metropolitics in motion: The dynamics of transportation and state reterritorialization in the Chicago and Toronto city-regions. *Urban Geography*, 34(2), 188–217.

Anderlini, Jamil. (2019). *How China's smart-city tech focuses on its own citizens.* Retrieved 1 October, 2019, from www.ft.com/content/46bc137a-5d27-11e9-840c-530737425559

Barrionuevo, J. M., Berrone, P., & Ricart, J. E. (2012). Smart cities, sustainable progress. *IESE Insight* 14, 50–57.

Buhalis, D. (2000). Marketing the competitive destination of the future. *Tourism Management*, 21(1), 97–116.

Chen, C. L. (2012). Reshaping Chinese space-economy through high-speed trains: opportunities and challenges. *Journal of Transport Geography*, 22(C), 312–316.

Cohen, B., (2012). *What Exactly is a Smart City? In Co.Exist*, Retrieved 21 October, 2019, from www.fastcoexist.com/1680538/what-exactly-is-a-smart-city.

Gandy, M. (2003). Concrete and clay: reworking nature in New York City. London: MIT Press.

Giffinger, R., Fertner, C., Kramar, H., Kalasek, R., Pichler-Milanović, N., & Meijers, E. (2007). Smart cities: Ranking of European medium-sized cities. Vienna, Austria: Centre of regional science (srf), Vienna university of technology. Retrieved 1 October, 2019, from www.smart-cities.eu/download/smart_cities_final_report.pdf.

Harrison, C., Eckman, B., Hamilton, R., Hartswick, P., Kalagnanam, J., Paraszczak, J., & Williams, P. (2010). Foundations for smarter cities. *IBM Journal of Research and Development*, 54(4), 1–16.

He, K., Huo, H., & Zhang, Q. (2002). Urban air pollution in China: current status, characteristics, and progress. *Annual Review of Energy and the Environment*, 27(1), 397–431.

Hong Kong 2030+. (2017). *Hong Kong 2030: Planning Vision and Strategy.* Retrieved 1 October, 2019, from www.hk2030plus.hk/about_a.htm

Huang, X. K., Yuan, J. Z., & Shi, M. Y. (2012, December). Condition and key issues analysis on the smarter tourism construction in China. *In International Conference on Multimedia and Signal Processing* (pp. 444–450). Berlin: Springer.

Lee, J. H., Phaal, R., & Lee, S. H. (2013). An integrated service-device-technology roadmap for smart city development. Technological Forecasting and Social Change, 80(2), 286–306.

Levinson, D. M. (2012). Accessibility impacts of high speed rail. Journal of Transport Geography, 22, 288–291.

McKinsey & Company (2011). *Urban world: Mapping the economic power of cities.* Retrieved 1 October, 2019, from www.mckinsey.com/~/media/mckinsey/featured%20insights/urbanization/urban%20world/mgi_urban_world_mapping_economic_power_of_cities_full_report.ashx

MTR Corporation Limited (2019). *High Speed Rail.* Retrieved 1 October, 2019, from www.highspeed.mtr.com.hk/en/about/hsr-intro.html

Ritchie, J. B., & Crouch, G. I. (2003). *A model of destination competitiveness. The competitive destination: a sustainable tourism perspective*, 60–78. Wallingford: CABI.

Rodrigue, J. P., Comtois, C., & Slack, B. (2017*). The geography of transport systems* (4th Ed.). New York: Routledge.

UBS. (2018). *China's cities of tomorrow feature some pretty jaw-dropping technologies.* Retrieved 1 December 2018, from https://mashable.com/2018/01/08/china-cities-of-the-future/#bwhTmsqlKsq9

6 Residents' attitude towards city integration and tourism development in the Greater Bay Area

Introduction

Greater Bay Area (GBA)

Globalization has facilitated the integration of cities, regions, and countries to form large-scale urbanized areas. These areas eventually become the building blocks of the global economy (Hui, Li, Chen, & Lang, 2018). The thirteenth Five-Year Plan for Economic and Social Development of the People's Republic of China (2016–2020) aims to increase the level of integration and encourages economic development by introducing the GBA (CPC central government, 2016). The inclusion of the GBA into the thirteenth Five-Year Plan shows that the GBA is part of the national strategy (CPC central government, 2019). The idea of forming a bay area by incorporating the PRD and the two SARs was originally introduced by academia. This cognition-deepening and these connotation-enriching ideas eventually spread to and are recognized by government officials and are implemented (Wang, 2018).

The GBA is located on the southeast coast of China. Geographically, it is close to the areas of Pearl River Bay, the Dapeng Bay, and the Daya Bay. The GBA comprises of nine cities from Guangdong and two SARs. The nine cities from Guangdong are Guangzhou, Shenzhen, Zhuhai, Dongguan, Foshan, Jiangmen, Zhaoqing, Zhongshan, and Huizhou. The two SARs are Hong Kong and Macau (Govada & Rodgers, 2019). The total area of the GBA is more than 56,000 km². The land size represents around 1 per cent of land in China (Yang & Li, 2019). The total population in the same area is roughly 66 million, which indicates around 5 per cent of the people in China reside in this area (Lin, Chen, Han, Chen, & Li, 2019). The World Bank estimated that the GBA is the largest urban area in the world regardless of land size, population, and economic output.

The GBA can be broadly classified into three metropolitan areas. Hong Kong and Shenzhen are considered as one, Guangzhou and Foshan are regarded as second, and Macau and Zhuhai are considered as third (Govada & Rodgers, 2019). These three areas are the drivers of economic growth and where most people are located or plan to migrate to. The GDP of the GBA in 2018 was over 10 trillion RMB, which is more than the GDP of South Korea in the same year (Southern Metropolis Daily, 2019). Lin et al. (2019) pointed out that the GBA is not only merely combining several cities together, but also developing a region with strong economic foundation, unique geographical location, complete infrastructure and industrial base, convenient transportation and global financial centre status.

Tourism development in the GBA

The formation of the GBA helps improve the economy of all cities in the region, given that tourism is a part of the economy, tourism is also developing hand-in-hand as the economy grows (Zeng, 2018). When the GBA is established, the tourism resources between all cities begin to complement each other with a solid foundation and good co-operation. The number of tourists and the amount of tourism revenue in the GBA increased more than five times between 2005 and 2017 (see Figure 6.1).

Gao (2019) believed that the GBA is a mature and well-developed tourism area. The introduction of the GBA enhances tourism development. Gao (2019) also cited the Outline of the PRD Regional Reform and

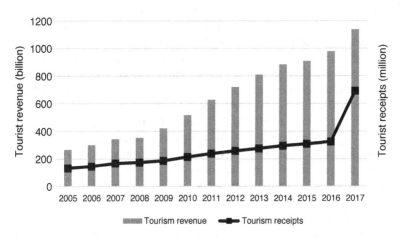

Figure 6.1 Tourism revenue and tourist receipts in Greater Bay Area (2005–2017).

Development Plan, the Guangdong–Hong Kong Cooperation Framework Agreement and the Guangdong–Macau Co-operation Framework Agreement as examples. Feng (2018) reported five new tourism products combining Guangdong, Hong Kong and Macau. These products contain different characteristics or themes. Some products focus on food, shopping, and the beach, whereas other products focus on heritage, culture, and root seeking. The GBA Tourism Industry Co-operation Agreement aims to promote the development of tourism resources in the GBA and achieve advantage complementation (Liu, 2017). The first general meeting of GBA Urban Tourism Association was held in Guangzhou, 10 special tourist routes in the GBA were launched at the conference, covering historical and cultural tourism, and overseas study tour (Ding, 2018). The development plan for the GBA was officially issued in February 2019. The purpose of the plan is to promote tourism development in the GBA, enrich tourism routes of the GBA and develop more tourism products of multidestination travel (Tian, 2019).

Literature review

Metropolitan regions

China is one of the most urbanized countries in the world. The metropolitan areas in China can dominate the national economic spatial pattern (Lu, Li, & Sun, 2003). The metropolitan area was originally linked to the PRD, the Yangtze River Delta, or the Greater Jakarta in Indonesia, which are all in east Asia (McGee & Robinson, 1995; Hall, 1999). Lottier (1938) defined a metropolitan area as an area with a dominating central city surrounded by several satellite cites. Hall (2009) defined it as a new form of urban area. It is an urban area with high population density and multiple scales of cities. The cities in the region/area are closely linked, regardless of terms of location or functions. The close connection between cities allows them to complement each other's strength and achieve a new type of division of labour. Scott (2001) described a metropolitan area as a large-scale urbanized area with important contributions to the economy in the region, the country and the world. Despite economic contributions, the metropolitan area would increase the level of innovation in the region and hence increase competitiveness (Li, Sun, & Li, 2010).

China has 13 metropolitan areas, namely, Beijing–Tianjin–Hebei, Yangtze River Delta and PRD in the eastern region, Jinzhong in the central region, Chengyu, Guanzhong, Beibu Gulf, Central Yunnan, Central Guizhou, Lanzhou–Xining, Ningxia and the Northern Tianshan Slope in the western region, and Hachang in the northeast region (Wang, Wang,

Chen, & Xu, 2019). Among these metropolitan areas, Beijing–Tianjin–Hebei, Yangtze River Delta, and the PRD are the three most mature metropolitan areas in China (Ye, Zhu, Li, Yang & Chen, 2019). These metropolitan areas are mature in terms of cities' scale, functions, population intensity, and industrial development level. The GBA is an extension of the PRD with increased and innovative co-operation mechanism and cross-boundary infrastructure development (Hui, Li, Chen, & Lang, 2018). An important difference of the GBA with the rest of the bay areas in the world is 'one country, two systems' and three tariff zones (Liu, 2017).

Resident attitude towards tourism development

Some researchers have investigated residents attitudes toward tourism development due to its close relationship with tourism development (Johnson, 1997). Attitude is defined as the psychological state of individuals. The psychological state, although is affected by values and personalities, is reinforced by perception in the real world (Getz, 1994). Previous research has found significant differences in residents' attitude towards tourism development. However, these studies usually merely examined the perceived tourism impact (Gursoy, Ouyang, Nunkoo, & Wei, 2018).

On the one hand, several researchers discovered that people have positive attitude towards tourism development. Tournois and Djeric (2018) found that most residents perceived that among all impacts of tourism development, economic, social-cultural, and environmental impacts are ranked first, second, and third, respectively. In addition, people expect when tourism development creates a positive impact on the economy, more jobs will be created, the living standard will be increased, and local economy will grow, therefore, economic impact is the most vital. Social-cultural impacts increase cultural activities, recreational facilities, community spirit, and exposure to other cultures, so they are ranked second. Gursoy et al. (2018) found that the perception of tourism impacts of people towards tourism development is also crucial. When people expect a positive impact of tourism development, they will have a positive attitude. However, when people expect a negative impact of tourism development, they will not support the tourism development. Similar to Tournois and Djeric (2018), Gursoy et al. (2018) not only discovered that economic impact is the most important, but also the ranking of the top-three impacts. Chen and Chen (2010) investigated residents' attitudes towards tourism development through structural equation modelling and the findings revealed that residents support for tourism development due to the perceived positive impact of tourism development is far greater than its negative tourism impact. Andereck, Valentine, Knopf, and Vogt (2015) also uncovered similar results.

On the other hand, some researchers have found negative attitudes. Tournois and Djeric (2018) discovered that because environmental impacts increase pollution, traffic jams, noise, overcrowding, wildlife destruction, and vandalism, it is the third most important impact affecting people's attitude towards tourism development. Other researchers indicated that the negative impact of tourism development may even 'cancel out' positive impacts, such as increase in living standards (Gursoy, Jurowski, & Uysal, 2002; Harrill & Potts, 2003). Chen and Chen (2010) reported that although tourism development may provide positive impact towards the economy, other economic problems, such as increase in crime rate, tax burden, and asset prices, also arise. Andereck et al. (2015) found similar results.

Sustainable development theory

Sustainable development theory classified residents' attitude towards tourism development into economic, social cultural, and environmental. This theory is originally proposed by the World Commission on Environment and Development in 1987. They defined sustainable development as a compromise between the needs of the current population and demands of future generations (UNWCED, 1987). In 1992, the Agenda 21 signed by 102 Head of States in the United Nations of Conference on Environmental and Development further confirmed the classifications (International Council for Local Environmental Initiative, 1996). To incorporate sustainable development into practice was important if one decided to follow a sustainable direction (Luo, 2018).

Framework of the study

As the above literature reviews suggested, the resident's attitude towards tourism development can be classified into perceived economic impacts, perceived socio-cultural impacts, and perceived environmental impacts. These dimensions are listed in Table 6.1. These dimensions are further classified into two sub-dimensions, namely, positive and negative impacts. These dimensions and sub-dimensions are combined to develop a framework.

Method

The purpose of this research is to explore residents' attitudes towards tourism development in the GBA. This research adopted a qualitative

Table 6.1 Proposed theoretical framework

Dimensions	Theoretical support
1 Perceived economic impacts *Positive* • Driving local economic growth • Promoting local tourism products • Raising the level of residents' life *Negative* • Increasing residents' living costs • Commercialization of tourist attractions	McCool & Martin, 1994; Lankford, 1994; Harrill & Potts, 2003; Huang, Gu & Yuan, 2008; Chen & Chen, 2010; Andereck, Valentine, Knopf & Vogt, 2015; Gursoy, Ouyang, Nunkoo & Wei, 2018; Tournois & Djeric, 2018.
2 Perceived socio-cultural impacts *Positive* • Increasing cross-cultural communication • Increasing local cultural identity *Negative* • Increasing crime rates • Increasing conflicts between tourists and residents	Harrill & Potts, 2003; Huang, Gu & Yuan, 2008; Chen & Chen, 2010; Andereck, Valentine, Knopf & Vogt, 2015; Tournois & Djeric, 2018.
3 Perceived environmental impacts *Positive* • Increasing more infrastructures • Making transports more convenient *Negative* • Crowding of public facilities and resources • Causing environment pollution • Destroying the lifestyle of residents	Lankford, 1994; Lindberg & Johnson, 1997; Teye, Sonmez & Sirakaya, 2002; Harrill & Potts, 2003; Huang, Gu & Yuan, 2008; Chen & Chen,2010; Andereck, Valentine, Knopf & Vogt, 2015.

research method. This method does not require any statistic techniques and is used in many studies to identify variables, which cannot be identified by quantitative methods (Strauss & Corbin, 1998).

This research collected the sample by convenient sampling. 18 residents from the GBA were selected as the interviewees of this study. The interviews were conducted from July–September 2019. Chinese and English were available to the interviewees, although most interviewees decided to use Chinese. Because this study aims to identify residents' attitudes towards tourism development in the GBA, a semi-structured interview questionnaire with open-ended questions was adopted in this study. There are two sections in the questionnaire. The first section contains questions related to residents' attitudes towards tourism development in the GBA.

The second section collects the demographic profiles of the interviewees. All questions in the interview were designed based on the existing literature and were reviewed by two researchers. The questions in the interview included the following: (1) In your opinion, what are the city integration factors that may influence tourism development in China? (2) What are the effects of city integration towards tourism development of the GBA including regional and city level?

The average duration of the interviews was 20 minutes. The entire interview was recorded to collect the answers of the questions. To ensure accuracy, the interviews were immediately transcribed and then sent to the interviewees to verify the contents' accuracy (Mabuza, Govender, Ogunbanjo, & Mash, 2014). Thereafter, the back-to-back method was used to translate the transcripts of the interviews. The corresponding information was inputted into NVivo 12.0 for further analysis after the interviews were recorded, transcribed, and translated. Two researchers worked co-operatively. The two researchers of the study examined the transcript individually. They first examined the transcript and then developed a framework. Thereafter, the researchers discussed their findings. The above process will repeat until they reach an agreement. Content analysis is used in this research. Given that content analysis provides opportunities for researchers to access the transcript and content independently, they are less influenced by existing theories or concepts. The results, which are revealed in this study are open to discussion (Jennings, 2001). In addition, the researchers agreed that consistent and similar results were found. To ensure accuracy, three more interviews were conducted to confirm the consistency. No new information was found from these three interviews. This study conducted 18 interviews.

Results

Characteristics of the interviewees

This study used semi-structured interviews to identify residents' attitudes towards tourism development in the GBA. A total of 18 interviewees participated in the interviews; all of the interviewees were residents from the GBA. Of the respondents, there were 11 males and seven females. The number of respondents aged between 18 to 24, 25 to 34, 35 to 44, 45 to 54, 55 to 64, and above 65 are 4, 6, 4, 2, 1, and 1, respectively. Six interviewees were from Macau, other interviewees were from Zhuhai, Foshan, Zhongshan, Dongguan, Hong Kong, Zhaoqing, Guangzhou, and Shenzhen. The proportions of working staffs, students, and retirees were 72 per cent, 22 per cent, and 6 per cent. The proportions of interviewees with high school, diploma, bachelor, and master were 6 per cent, 17 per cent, 33 per cent, and 44 per cent respectively. The 15 interviewees have resided in the GBA for over 20 years. Thus, this sample should sufficiently represent the residents from the GBA. A summary of the demographic information of the interviewees can be found in Table 6.2.

Findings from interview results

One question asked was 'In your opinion, what are the city integration factors that may influence tourism development in China?' This question aimed to identify residents' attitudes towards tourism development in the GBA. The literature review shows that residents' attitude towards tourism development can be classified into perceived economic impacts, perceived socio-cultural impacts and perceived environmental impacts. The results shown in Table 6.3 indicate six common residents' attitudes: perceived positive economic impacts, perceived negative economic impacts, perceived positive socio-cultural impacts, perceived negative socio-cultural impacts, perceived positive environmental impacts, and perceived negative environmental impacts. This section investigated each attitude accordingly.

Table 6.2 Demographic information of interviewees

No.	Sex	Age	City	Position	Level of education	Living in Greater Bay Area (Years)
1	M	35–44	Foshan	Working	Diploma	37
2	F	18–24	Zhuhai	Student	Master	2
3	F	35–44	Foshan	Working	Master	40
4	M	18–24	Macau	Student	Bachelor	23
5	M	25–34	Foshan	Working	Bachelor	28
6	F	65+	Macau	Retire	High School	67
7	F	25–34	Zhongshan	Working	Master	25
8	F	25–34	Dong Guan	Working	Diploma	7
9	M	35–44	Macau	Working	Bachelor	35
10	M	35–44	Zhuhai	Working	Master	2
11	M	55–64	Hong Kong	Working	Bachelor	55
12	M	45–54	Macau	Working	Bachelor	46
13	M	45–54	Zhaoqing	Working	Master	45
14	F	25–34	Macau	Student	Master	25
15	F	18–24	Guangzhou	Student	Master	24
16	M	25–34	Macau	Working	Master	25
17	M	18–24	Shenzhen	Working	Bachelor	24
18	M	25–34	Zhuhai	Working	Diploma	28

Table 6.3 Results of content analysis

Attitudes	Sub-attitudes	Frequency count
Perceived positive economic impacts	Driving local economic growth	6
	Promoting local tourism products	14
	Raising the level of residents' life	8
Perceived negative economic impacts	Increasing residents' living costs	8
	Commercialization of tourist attractions	5
Perceived positive socio-cultural impacts	Increasing cross-cultural communication	17
	Increasing local cultural identity	6
Perceived negative socio-cultural impacts	Increasing crime rates	6
	Increasing conflicts between tourists and residents	23
Perceived positive environmental impacts	Increasing more infrastructures	6
	Making transports more convenient	30
Perceived negative environmental impacts	Crowding of public facilities and resources	6
	Causing environment pollution	7
	Destroying the lifestyle of residents	8

Perceived positive economic impacts

The dimension of perceived positive economic impacts was mentioned 28 times. The perceived positive economic impacts have three sub-dimensions: driving local economic growth, promoting local tourism products, and raising the level of residents' life. First, driving local economic growth is one of the residents' attitudes under the dimension of perceived positive economic impacts. One interviewee said that 'the development of tourism has driven the economy of small cities, more and more tourists tend to visit small cities, which have not been developed and urbanised' (Interviewee 14). Another interviewee mentioned that 'tourism development has a positive effect on the city's economy, including promoting closer economic connections between cities in the GBA and helping the fast development of networks economy' (Interviewee 9). Second, promoting local tourism products is another crucial sub-attitude identified. One interviewee stated that:

> the development of tourism in the GBA makes it easier for people to buy local souvenirs, for example, it is very convenient for us to travel to Hong Kong, we could go back and forth in a day, so we just bought some special local products and then went back.
>
> (Interviewee 1)

Another interviewee said, 'tourism attractions in small cities have been developed and promoted due to tourism development' (Interviewee 14). Third, raising the level of residents' life is one of sub-attitudes that can reflect residents' views on tourism development in the GBA. As one interviewee mentioned,

> the development of tourism in the GBA has made our life more diverse and convenient, for example, I went to a place to have morning tea, and then I went to another place to visit the park in the evening, all of these activities in our life can be achieved.
>
> (Interviewee 7)

Perceived negative economic impacts

The dimension of perceived negative economic impacts, which was mentioned 13 times, can be further divided into two sub-dimensions: increase of residents' living costs and commercialization of tourist attractions. First, increasing residents' living costs is a main resident concern in relation to tourism management under the dimension of perceived negative economic impacts. According to one interviewee, 'the prices are rising quickly because of the development of tourism and economy' (Interviewee 14). As stated by one interviewee, 'the prices of accommodation and meals has become very expensive' (Interviewee 17). Second, commercialization of tourist attractions is another important sub-attitude that can reflect residents' perspectives on tourism development in the GBA. Another interviewee said, 'nowadays, Macau's tourist attractions are too commercialised to visit, which leads us old with no places to go' (Interviewee 6). Another interviewee mentioned that 'after the economy of small cities is driven by the tourism industry, their tourist attractions will lose their original appearance and characteristics' (Interviewee 14).

Perceived positive socio-cultural impacts

The dimension of perceived positive socio-cultural impacts was mentioned 23 times. This dimension has two sub-dimensions: increasing cross-cultural communication and increasing local cultural identity. First, increasing cross-cultural communication is a sub-attitude under the dimension of perceived positive socio-cultural impacts. According to one respondent, 'the development of tourism allows people to have more opportunities to visit other cities in the GBA and people can learn more about the culture of other cities' (Interviewee 17). Another respondent mentioned that 'Guangdong belongs to Lingnan culture, Macau belongs to entertainment culture and Hong Kong belongs to local culture, three different cultures can be complemented through the development of tourism' (Interviewee 18). Second, increasing local cultural identity is another main sub-attitude that can reflect residents' attitudes towards tourism development. As one respondent stated, 'many people from Hong Kong and Macau have migrated from Guangdong, thus, the cultures and customs of the cities in GBA are similar, and tourism development will lead people to recognise cultural identity' (Interviewee 3).

Perceived negative socio-cultural impacts

The dimension of perceived negative socio-cultural impacts was mentioned 29 times. Rising crime rates and increasing conflicts between tourists and residents are grouped under this dimension. For rising crime rates, one response indicated that 'safety is the most important thing for our life, but the tourism development has led to an increase in crime rate and a decrease in security guarantee' (Interviewee 6). Another interviewee said, 'the mobility of population is large due to the development of tourism, which is harmful to the security and stability' (Interviewee 13). For increasing conflicts between tourists and residents, as one interviewee stated, 'the phenomenon of conflicts between the local culture and the foreign culture is very common in the process of tourism development, the local culture sometimes will be impacted by the foreign culture when the foreign culture is too strong' (Interviewee 11). In addition, one interviewee mentioned that 'there are differences in culture and customs between different cities in the GBA, thus, tourism development not only provides communication opportunities for people in different cities, but also creates conflicts' (Interviewee 16).

Perceived positive environmental impacts

The dimension of perceived positive environmental impacts, mentioned 36 times, can be further sub-divided into two: increasing more infrastructures and making transports more convenient. For increasing more infrastructures, one respondent said, 'the government began to pay attention to the construction of infrastructure facilities due to the development of tourism' (Interviewee 14). Another respondent mentioned that 'formalities for customs clearance are simplified with the development of tourism, for instance, it is very convenient for us to go to Macau because of the fast customs clearance' (Interviewee 13). For making transports more convenient, as stated by one respondent, 'tourism development has made transportation more convenient, for example, it used to take a few hours to get a place by cars or boats, now it can be reached by light rails in an hour' (Interviewee 1). Another respondent stated that 'the construction and opening of the Hong Kong-Zhuhai-Macau Bridge should be the result of tourism development' (Interviewee 3).

Perceived negative environmental impacts

The dimension of perceived negative environmental impacts was mentioned 21 times. Crowding of public facilities and resources, causing environment pollution and destroying the lifestyle of residents are grouped under this dimension. First, crowding of public facilities and resources is a sub-attitude under the perceived negative environmental impacts. As one interviewee stated, 'some cities may have a large floating population due to tourism development, thus, the public resources and facilities are strained' (Interviewee 17). Second, causing environment pollution is one of sub-attitudes that can reflect residents' views on tourism development in the GBA according to one interviewee, 'tourism development has a great impact on the environment, especially the pollution problem' (Interviewee 8). Third, destroying the lifestyle of residents is one of the residents' attitudes under the dimension of perceived negative environmental impacts. One interviewee mentioned that 'the phenomenon of different lifestyles and personal habits between residents and tourists is the result of tourism development, which would spoil local residents' way of life with the growing influx of tourists' (Interviewee 12). As stated by another interviewee, 'different culture, history, tradition, values, ways of life, habits and customs exist in different cities, which may lead to conflicts in the process of tourism development' (Interviewee 16).

Conclusions and limitations

The results revealed that residents' attitudes towards tourism development in the GBA can be divided into six dimensions, namely, perceived positive economic impacts, perceived negative economic impacts, perceived positive socio-cultural impacts, perceived negative socio-cultural impacts, perceived positive environmental impacts and perceived negative environmental impacts. After analysing the frequency count of the six dimensions on residents' attitudes, the dimension of perceived positive environmental impacts was the most important one that reflect residents' views on tourism development in the GBA, followed by the perceived negative socio-cultural impacts and perceived positive economic impacts.

In summary, the perceived positive environmental impacts, perceived negative socio-cultural impacts and perceived positive economic impacts were the top three important attitudes of residents towards tourism development in the GBA. The findings of study are basically consistent with those of previous research about residents' attitude towards tourism development. The findings also provide new insights into the literature about residents' attitude towards tourism development.

This study is a preliminary attempt to identify the main residents' attitudes towards tourism development in the GBA by analysing the related literature and collected records. However, this study has several limitations that require further investigation. First, this study only adopts the qualitative method along with semi-structured interview. Future studies can use the combination of qualitative and quantitative research methods. Second, this study only focuses on residents' attitudes. The attitudes of tourists and the government are excluded, and, thus, future studies can explore these stakeholders. Third, this study aims to explore the tourism development of the GBA. The results may not represent the tourism development in other regions. Future studies can investigate the tourism development in other regions, such as Beijing–Tianjin–Hebei and Yangtze River Delta.

References

Andereck, K. L., Valentine, K. M., Knopf, R. C. & Vogt, C. A. (2015) Residents' perceptions of community tourism impact. *Annals of Tourism Research*, 32(4), 1056–1076.

Chen, C. F., & Chen, P. C. (2010). Resident attitudes toward heritage tourism development. *Tourism Geographies*, 12(4), 525–545.

CPC central government (2016). The 13th Five-Year Plan for Economic and Social Development of the People's Republic of China (2016–2020). Retrieved 24 October 2019, from www.gov.cn/xinwen/2016-03/17/content_5054992.htm

CPC central government (2019). The Development Plan for Guangdong–Hong Kong–Macau Greater Bay Area. Retrieved 24 October 2019, from www.gov.cn/zhengce/2019-02/18/content_5366593.htm#1

Ding, Chi. (2018, June). Exploring the multi destination travel tourism market in Guangdong–Hong Kong–Macau Greater Bay Area. *Time Weekly*. Retrieved 25 September 2019, from www.time-weekly.com/html/20180619/251765_1.html

Feng, Y. Q. (2018). Tourism revenue exceeds trillions, Guangdong–Hong Kong–Macau Greater Bay Area expand multi destination travel new market. Retrieved 25 September 2019, from www.yicai.com/news/5430461.html

Gao, T. (2019). A Review of Research on Tourism Integration in Guangdong–Hong Kong–Macau Greater Bay Area. *Advances in Social Science, Education and Humanities Research*, 344, 253–262.

Getz, D. (1994). Residents' attitudes towards tourism development: A longitudinal study in Spey Valley, Scotland. *Tourism Management*, 15(4), 247–258.

Govada, S. S., & Rodgers, T. (2019). Towards Smarter Regional Development of Hong Kong Within the Greater Bay Area. In T. M. Vinod Kumar (ed.), *Smart Metropolitan Regional Development* (pp. 101–171). Springer Nature Singapore Pte Ltd.

Gursoy, D., Jurowski, C., & Uysal, M. (2002). Resident attitudes. *Annals of Tourism Research*, 29(1), 79–105.

Gursoy, D., Ouyang, Z., Nunkoo, R., & Wei, W. (2018). Residents' impact perceptions of and attitudes towards tourism development: a meta-analysis. *Journal of Hospitality Marketing & Management*, 1–28.

Hall, P. (1999). Planning for the mega-city: A new eastern Asian urban form? In J. Brotchie, P. Newton, P. Hall, & J. Dickey (Eds). *East west perspectives on 21st century urban development: Sustainable eastern and western cities in the new millennium*. Aldershot: Ashgate.

Hall, P. (2009). Looking backward, looking forward: The city region of the mid-21st century. *Regional Studies*, 43(6), 803–817.

Harrill, R., & Potts, T. D. (2003). Tourism planning in historic districts: Attitudes toward tourism development in Charleston. *Journal of the American Planning Association*, 69(3), 233–244.

Hui, C. M., Li, X., Chen, T., & Lang, W. (2018). Deciphering the spatial structure of China's megacity region: A new bay area – The Guangdong–Hong Kong–Macau Greater Bay Area in the making. *Cities*, in press. https://doi.org/10.1016/j.cities.2018.10.011

International Council for Local Environmental Initiative (1996). *The Local Agenda 21 Planning Guide: An Introduction to Sustainable Development Planning*. ICLEE.

Jennings, G. (2001). *Tourism research*. Milton, QLD: John Wiley and Sons Australia, Ltd.

Lankford, S. V. (1994). Attitudes and perceptions toward tourism and rural regional development. *Journal of Tourism Research*, 32(3), 35–43.

Li, J. M., Sun, T. S., Li, G. P. (2010). Comparative study of the division of Labor and its complementarity in three major metropolitan regions of China. *Scientia Geographica Sinica*, 30(4), 503–509.

Lin, X., Chen, D., Han, J., Chen, T., & Li, C. (2019). A Study on the Role of Guangdong–Hong Kong–Macau Greater Bay Area Based on the Belt and Road Initiative. *Journal of Economics and Business*, 2(3), 722–738.

Liu, X. T. (2017). Tourism development in Guangdong–Hong Kong–Macau Greater Bay Area welcomes new opportunities. Retrieved 28 September 2019, from http://news.163.com/17/1222/08/D68DS71D00014AEE.html

Lottier, S. (1938). Distribution of criminal offenses in metropolitan regions. *Journal of Criminal Law and Criminology* (1931–1951), 29(1), 37–50.

Lu, M. H., Li, G. P., & Sun, T. S. (2003). Research on Functional Division among the Core Cities in Tokyo Megalopolis and Its Enlightenment. *Scientia Geographica Sinica*, 23(2), 150–156.

Luo, J. M. (2018). A Measurement Scale of Corporate Social Responsibility in Gambling Industry from Customer Perspective. *Journal of Quality Assurance in Hospitality & Tourism*, 19(4), 461–476.

Mabuza, L. H., Govender, I., Ogunbanjo, G. A., & Mash, B. (2014). African Primary Care Research: Qualitative data analysis and writing results. *Afr. J. Prim. Health Care Fam. Med.* 6, 1–5.

McGee, T. G., & Robinson, I. (Eds). (1995). *The mega-urban regions of Southeast Asia.* Vancouver, BC: University of British Columbia Press.

Scott, A. J. (2001). Globalization and the rise of city-regions. *European Planning Studies*, 9(7), 813–826.

Southern Metropolis Daily (2019). GDP data of cities in the Guangdong–Hong Kong–Macau greater bay area in 2018. Retrieved 25 October 2019, from www.sohu.com/a/296338727_124712

Strauss, A., & Corbin, J. (1998). *Basics of Qualitative Research: Procedures and Techniques for Developing Grounded Theory.* Thousand Oaks, CA: Sage.

Tian, H. (2019). Building a world-class destination is the 'new power' for the development of the cultural tourism industry in Guangdong–Hong Kong–Macau Greater Bay Area. Retrieved 28 September 2019, from http://travel.people.com.cn/n1/2019/0222/c41570-30897670.html

Tournois, L., & Djeric, G. (2018). Evaluating urban residents' attitudes towards tourism development in Belgrade (Serbia). *Current Issues in Tourism*, 19, 1–9.

United Nations World Commission on Environment and Development (UNWCED). (1987), *Our Common Future (The Brundtland Report).* Oxford: Oxford University Press.

Wang, F. Q. (2018). Guangdong–Hong Kong–Macau Greater Bay Area and the development opportunities in Macau. *Administration*, 31(119), 5–10.

Wang, D. L., Wang, Y., Chen, Y., & Xu, J. (2019). Analysis on the evolution characteristics and laws of urban scale distribution in China's urban agglomeration. *Ecological Economy*, 35(2), 95–100.

World Bank (2017). World Bank report provides new data to help ensure urban growth benefits the poor. Retrieved 25 October 2019, from www.worldbank.org/en/news/press-release/2015/01/26/world-bank-report-provides-new-data-to-help-ensure-urban-growth-benefits-the-poor

Yang, D., & Li, C. (2019). Study on the Spatial Pattern of Innovation Output and Influencing Factors in Guangdong–Hong Kong–Macau Greater Bay Area. Retrieved 25 October 2019, from www.preprints.org/manuscript/201905.0268/v1

Ye, C., Zhu, J., Li, S., Yang, S., & Chen, M. (2019). Assessment and analysis of regional economic collaborative development within an urban agglomeration: Yangtze River Delta as a case study. Habitat International, 83, 20-29.

Zeng, L. (2018). Study on the efficiency and the cooperative direction of tourism and leisure industry in Guangdong–Hong Kong–Macau greater bay area. *Open Journal of Social Sciences*, 06(1), 93–105.

Index

Printed in the United States
by Baker & Taylor Publisher Services